LEMON Leadership®

Radically fresh leadership

Published by
Indaba Publishing, California
A division of
The Institute for Innovation, Integration & Impact, Inc.
www.inst.net

Telephone: 1-866-9-INDABA
www.indabapublishing.com

ISBN 0-9678541-3-X

Graphics and book design by
Brett Johnson, Jnr. (brett@insprung.com)

To the LEMONs who live with me.

LEMON Leadership®

Radically fresh leadership

by

Brett Johnson

www.lemonleadership.com

Published by Indaba Publishing

Contact information:

brett@inst.net

Why another book about leadership?

My work involves meeting with many leaders from around the world each year, and they have this in common: they all want to have an impact. They have mastered their craft and moved beyond the basics of running an organization. Best Practices are routine. They are looking at the deeper life issues. This inevitably brings them to the topic of leadership, and more specifically, who they are.

This book is not a "How To" of leadership, but a "Who are you?" book that considers leadership in a fresh way. Those who work at the coalface of human need are convinced that the lack of leaders is the number one issue in the world today. This stems partly from the fact that our definitions of leadership are too narrow – incomplete. We know lots about entrepreneurs and managers, but there are other types of leaders about which we know precious little. LEMON Leadership® expands our view of leadership to cover five distinct types of leaders; not styles, not temperaments, not preferences… types.

The simple truths about LEMON Leadership have transformed the lives of individual leaders and changed the working of executive teams. Understanding the truisms in this book will radically increase your impact.

This book has many generalizations and definite statements to which there are clear exceptions. If I paused to deal with the exceptions to every observation, this book would be twice as long and half as interesting.

Brett Johnson
Emerald Hills, California

PS: To those leaders who object to being thought of as a LEMON… lighten up – it will do wonders for your leadership.

Table of Contents

Chapter 9: Bitter LEMON – Weaknesses of LEMONs

Chapter 10: You say what you are – LEMON speak

Chapter 01
Five types of leaders

*H*ow did you happen upon these five types of leaders? Was there some empirical research, or is this just intuition? Let me answer this question with a story.

An extraordinary set of events steered a group of leaders from four different organizations into a real estate venture. With some excitement mixed with soul searching they decided to team up on what could be a multi-million dollar venture. Excited about the synergies of the organizations, they suspected that the definite gifts of the leaders of the various organizations would be a great plus. Each leader had twenty to thirty years of experience under his belt. They were passionate and had a strong sense of purpose. Perhaps most importantly, they had common values that could pave the way for good relationships, communication and decision-making. Things should have gone smoothly, but they didn't. I was one of the leaders, and on more than one occasion I found myself nonplussed by the perspectives of people whom I considered to be good friends, gifted individuals, and all-around great people. I observed what I perceived to be an inconsistency between reality as I saw it and actions from other leaders. Did we not believe the same things, have similar values, and profess shared goals? Were we not passionate about the same things? Faced with the challenges of understanding how people who were committed to me, my family, my business—people who wanted the best for me—could conduct themselves in a way that was somewhat inconceivable to my way of thinking, I had to conclude that there was some understanding of leadership that broke my past molds.

In the business world I might have explained this situation away as "swimming with the sharks" or "just the way business is done" or "if you can't stand the heat, stay out of the kitchen." But these trite sayings seemed less applicable because I knew the leaders involved to be people of high integrity. We talked, we wrestled with concepts, we dreamed about accomplishments, we laughed, and we cried. In short, we invested in relationships so that we had a solid foundation for working together. So what could explain the degeneration? Over time I began to understand that all the pieces of paper, the contracts, the vision statements, the prospectuses, and the business plans paled in comparison to one bigger factor that lay in the shadows, threatening our joint venture. I began to poke at it, name it, define it: each of the many things that we thought we had going for us was subject to a greater reality. Slowly the notions of LEMON Leadership began to take shape like people emerging from a morning mist. Initially they were just some ideas. Over the past seven years they have become clearer, sharper and more powerful. This month, this week—sometimes days in a row—I gain new insights. Reading this book will provide seed capital for your own journey of discovery. But I am getting ahead of the story.

Each of us leaders came from a corporate context that had its own influence on who we were as leaders. The values and operating principles of our corporations greatly influenced things. Some were for-profit corporations, and some were non-profit organizations. But this was not the key. Another influencing factor was the imperfections each of us brought to the table because we were not without our own blind spots. These two elements paled in comparison to the overriding reality of leadership DNA that affected the whole venture. Who we were as leaders colored more than we cared to know. Each of us was acting out of our identity as leaders more than out of anything to which we had agreed on paper or conceived of over many fine hours of dreaming.

Just how many types of leaders are there? Not styles, not personality traits, not Myers-Briggs profiles, but categories of leaders? Much has been written on leadership, and the more serious writings focus on two types of leaders: Managers and Entrepreneurs. There are books on variations of managers, such as General Managers, Business Managers, and Personal Managers, but the field of leadership literature categorizes leaders into these two broad boxes—Managers and Entrepreneurs—and then adds stylistic variations to explain differences such as:

- Direct, indirect
- Random, sequential
- Concrete, abstract
- Intuitive, analytical, etc., etc.

Then, to top it off, if someone is a little out of the box or creative or beyond the pale in some way, a catch-all that covers a plethora of quirks is added to this list: "Visionary."

> "She's an entrepreneur… real intuitive."
> "He's a manager… concrete, direct, analytical…
> a real manager."
> "She's interesting… a real visionary," which normally means
> she has some qualities that I cannot put my finger on, but
> she has notions about the future that sound plausible.

As I looked at our joint venture group it was easy to see that there were one or two managers and entrepreneurs. But there were others who were neither, and when I knew that I could not explain all of our behavior as intentionally malicious or deceitful or obstructive, I had to find another explanation.

Backing away from the immediate story for a moment, my own experience in management consulting has created wonderful opportunities to work closely with senior executives from FORTUNE 500 companies and with entrepreneurs in smaller organizations. My particular work in the 1980's in a field called Executive Information Systems caused me to become a student of how individual executives were wired. This influenced the way they viewed and used corporate information. The notion was that information needed to be delivered to executives—with the typical concentration span of a gnat—in a format that mirrored their view of the organization and the world in which it operated. In my first such venture we took the entire reporting package for a major international oil company and reduced it to one page. I knew that executives viewed the world through different lenses and that figuring out this lens was critical to being able to serve them the information they needed in a manner that made sense to their view of the world. What I had not figured out was that there were some predictable patterns for different types of leaders. Each executive information system we created had to be geared to a particular executive, and was therefore expensive and ultimately unsustainable.

In our own real estate story it was apparent as time went by that we had some disconnects between the leaders of the joint venture. We had a good division of responsibilities, but handoffs between executives were blocked. We had a detailed project plan, but no common glossary on what "complete" or "I've done it" meant. We now had a staff in place, a monthly payroll that was creeping upwards, and we were starting to lose momentum. Still we made collective promises, nodded our heads as one, and stated truths in unison, but there was no shared reality. In the face of this I began to formulate an understanding of the different types of leaders involved. Pretty soon I tested these concepts with leadership teams in corporations of many types. Community leaders, government leaders, and children took LEMON Leadership tests. Business leaders through to marriage and family counselors affirmed and employed the LEMON Leadership truisms, and they have been shared with and verified by people in many cultural settings.

A definition of LEMONs

I have determined that there are in fact five types of leaders.

Luminaries	People who see the world through the lens of ideas, viewpoints, intellectual constructs, the "Why."
Entrepreneurs	People who see the world through the lens of opportunity, immediate needs to be filled, the "When."
Managers	People who see the systems, the practical workings, the "How."
Organizers	People who see the world through the lens of tasks to be done, people to be served, the "What."
Networkers	People who see the world through the lens of webs to be woven, people to be connected, elements to be gathered, the "Who."

The DNA of the leader shapes the texture of organizations quite significantly. Put a little differently, the tone, organizational structure, communication patterns and entire modus operandi of a corporation—whether a business or non-profit entity—is very different depending on which of the LEMONs is at the helm. Boards and outgoing executives handling issues of succession intuitively know this to be the case. Most of them frame the issues in terms of corporate culture and what is needed at this time in the life of the corporation. I believe that what they are sensing is that when you change an M for an O or an L for an E or an E for an N, you effectively usher in a change to the entire operating model. The whole modus operandi shifts when a leader leads out of their identity, which a good leader will do, and that identity is different from a predecessor. Many boards would rather substitute a B+ manager with a B+ manager than run the risk of changing the type of leader at the helm. This short book will not deal in depth with the dynamics of succession, but you should be alerted to the fact that the LEMON-type plays a significant role in change. If not recognized, one runs into the unseen corporate brick wall at high speed.

LEMON TRUISM: Unless the LEMON Leadership type and the fundamentals of the operating model are in sync, the leader or the organization will fail.

I alert you to this truism up front because when we discuss each type of leader I will try to give you a word-taste of what it is like to work in an organization led by each of the LEMONs. The dysfunction we see in some organizations, families and businesses stems from a failure to grasp this truth.

Categorizing yourself too quickly

When I meet someone and we talk about LEMON Leadership or when I am working with a group of executives, they are quick to want to categorize themselves. I have found that we make some common mistakes when hastily pigeon-holing people:

- We confuse style with DNA. So I have said, "She is a quiet introvert, therefore she cannot be a Networker." Wrong.
- We say, "He is a visionary therefore he is a Luminary." Wrong again. Every leader has vision, it just looks very different for each type of leader, and the vision of a Luminary is easier to spot than the vision of an Organizer so we say, "She has vision, ergo she is a Luminary."
- I've heard it said, "She is a teacher, therefore she is a Luminary." Also wrong. I have met many gifted teachers who are able to communicate the ideas of others but do not generate fresh ideas in a way that the Luminary does.

Before exploring each type of leader—avoiding the temptation to declare who one is too early—I have to point out that each of us is obviously a composite of several leadership types. As we get into the heart of the book you will discover that your primary and secondary LEMON typing radically affects how you lead on a good day, and on a bad day. You will also discover that this is not a book that says, "I am an Entrepreneur, so take it or leave it!" Having understood the different leadership types, you will uncover keys to dealing with yourself and others in situations calling for different types of leaders. The art of leadership is to know what type of leader is needed in any situation, and then to be free to adjust accordingly.

Let's examine the characteristics of leadership for each type of leader.

Chapter 02
Luminaries

*I*deas have consequences. No one knows this better than the Luminary who believes that everything begins with and revolves around ideas. Luminaries are thought leaders, fresh thinkers who enthuse and empower others through the world of ideas.

Characteristics of Luminaries

Luminaries are able to intuitively envision future consequences of today's reality. They can take data points from various sources and envision the impacts for years to come. In 1965 Gordon Moore, a cofounder of Intel, stated that the number of transistors per integrated circuit would double every couple of years. This became known as Moore's Law, and nearly forty years later it has held true. Back then there were 2,250 transistors per integrated circuit: the Pentium 4 chips have 42,000,000. Moore is a Luminary in the technology field.

A good way to get a feel for LEMON Leadership is to contemplate what each leader perceives as the beginning or genesis of something. Asking the question, "How did this all start?" will shed some light on what type of leader you are seeking to understand. For the Luminaries, they believe that ideas precede activities. Things begin with thinking. The Luminary can see mental frameworks and assumptions and philosophical constructs as clearly as though they were made of steel. They are happy to start with the speck of an idea and build from there.

Luminaries are thought leaders. By this I mean that their thinking takes something that exists, finds the gaps, the implications, or the areas for improvement and moves it further down the road. They value concepts, mental constructs and philosophies. This doesn't mean that they are all impractical do-nothings. It would be a mistake to think that all Luminaries are abstract. I had a meeting with a Luminary and a Networker and watched with amazement as whole sentences were spoken without comprehension because the Luminary, while conceptual, was concrete, and the Networker talked primarily in his native abstracts. So I have met those who are concrete in their thought patterns and mental maps. Yet their view of reality is one in which principles dominate, and such principles are perceived very much by the mind.

Everyone sees reality differently. Max du Pree says, "The first job of a leader is to define reality." What he doesn't say is that reality is defined according to the DNA of the person making such a definition. Luminaries are as interested in the reality that could be than in the reality that someone else describes to them. Luminaries like to deal their own hand. If they cannot do this, they simply invent a new card game. This is particularly true where you have a Luminary-Entrepreneur combination, and new ideas that could be products or businesses (often based on intellectual products) emanate at a dozen a day.

Living involves leading. Leaders are only leaders when they have followers. One sure way to lose your followers is to ignore their depth of field. When you take a photograph you have several variables such as aperture, light and depth of field. The greater the depth of field, the more there is that stays in focus at once. LEMONs, like cameras, have the ability to keep things in focus with differing depth of field. Luminaries generally have an ability to keep things in focus for years, not just months, weeks or days. Not only is the flower in the foreground in focus, but the mountains in the distance are in sharp relief. Because Luminaries are often long-range thinkers they have learned that the outworking of ideas can last for years, decades, generations and centuries. In an era where society reinvents itself every few years and many products are obsolete as soon as they hit the shelves, it is hard for us to think in generations, let alone centuries. To the Luminary this is not hard because what is right in principle remains right for a long, long time. A skillful Luminary will understand the depth of field of the people she leads and speak not just to the long haul, but to the more immediate field of focus of others.

I asked a Luminary friend who is a leader in the biotechnology field, "What percentage of the work you do is intellect, and what percent is inspiration?" "It is 90% inspiration," was his reply. Many Luminaries synthesize data from all sorts of places and form an intuitive view of the future that is uncannily accurate. Are they prophets? Not all of them. Do they have some weird insights that they somehow intuit? Not usually. More often it is the ability to see principles at work in the past, understand today in light of such principles, and then make a clear statement about what this means for the future.

Luminary-led organizations

I mentioned earlier that the DNA of the leader shapes the texture of organizations quite significantly. This is no less true in a family than in a business or political party. When a political leader who is idea driven comes into his or her own, we get things like the Contract with America and other intellectually driven plans. When things didn't quite work out exactly as planned for Newt Gingrich, the retired politician became an academic, further underlining his Luminary leanings. What is it like to work in an organization led by a Luminary? Luminaries inspire organizations with the power of an idea. Steve Jobs was a young man with more than a business plan; he had a vision—some say an ideology—about changing the world. I can already hear you saying, "Yes, but he wasn't a good manager." No prizes for that realization. No matter how sound that observation seems from a Business 101 perspective, it makes little difference. The people working at Apple would not work for a Manager if you paid them. They were in for the ride with the Luminary who created an environment that had a buzz because of the power of the idea: computing for the common man.

By now you are asking yourself, "Why was Jobs more successful at Apple when he came back as a forty-something year old?" My view: he wasn't any less of a Luminary, but he now realized that he had to dial up some of the other aspects of LEMONs in order to be effective. He had seen how uncompromising vision could kill companies, so he was more willing to recognize the relevance of the Ms and Os of this world.

Contrast Apple with Microsoft. Bill Gates is also a Luminary; a key difference between his leadership journey and that of Steve Jobs is that Gates has been accompanied by Steve Ballmer who has, from the outset, brought other elements of leadership to the mix.

Luminaries are particularly prone to the age-old executive trait of dive-bombing—swooping down from 10,000 feet, meddling in some piece of the business, then soaring back up to executive heights. This is a bad habit that many executives have acquired. Luminaries, however, tend to stay "above" the practical day-to-day tasks of an organization. Some of the implications of this will be seen in the chapter on the Weaknesses of LEMONs.

This highlights a final characteristic of Luminaries that I want to touch on for the moment, namely, that they care more about the "Why" than the "How." "How" is just a detail, and they don't always notice or do details, unless they are an L-M or an L-O combination. More on that later.

What is work?

One of the fascinating things about LEMON Leadership is that there is a tendency for each of the leadership types to regard what the others do as "not real work." I remember an annual appraisal at Price Waterhouse when a partner in the office said, "I cannot decide whether you are a talker or a doer." For a Luminary the talking is the doing. As a child my father told me how he would sit in his chair at the office with his long legs stretched out to where size 14 shoes formed a large V through which he could view passers by. "What are you doing?" they would ask. "I am working," came his reply. He was an idea man, and as the Marketing Director for an apparel company in South Africa his job was to come up with ideas that would sell products. It seems his best ideas came when his feet were on the desk. To the passerby, that was not work.

Before I dive into what Luminaries consider to be work let me make this brief statement: You will save yourself a lot of heartache if you fully grasp that LEMONs each have radically different definitions of what constitutes actual, real work. Beyond that, they have an innate suspicion (and sometimes a firm belief) that what the other LEMONs do is not really work in the true sense of the word.

Let's look at an example of what different people consider to be work.

A Manager in accounting thinks that what salespeople do isn't real work; it's just schmoozing and taking orders. Budgets, plans, spreadsheets, accounting, annual reports—now that's real work.	Salespeople (often Networkers) think that their craft of identifying real needs, fitting products or services to that need, winning over customers, and keeping the customers happy in the face of competition is the real work. The rest is boring admin and number crunching (the stuff Managers do).
Entrepreneurs think that seeing an opportunity, finding the resources to pursue it, managing risk and getting the company structured correctly to be a lead player is real work.	Organizers think that opportunities come and go but the real work is finding office space, hiring people, setting up trade shows, and fighting fires that Entrepreneurs don't even know are aflame ... now that's real work.

If you want to be successful don't just try to find your definition of work so that you can defend it: make the leap to understanding that it is all work, it is all needed, it is all good. What's more, if you can get inside the head of your LEMON colleagues, especially the ones who are not wired like you, then you will understand how they see work. Then when they tell you, "I did the job! It is finished," you will know what that really means.

The flip side is also true: if you fail to appreciate the nature of work for the other LEMONs, then you will inevitably build a team that is devoid of key leadership types, the team will have blind spots at best, prejudices at worst, and will fail to deliver sustainable impact. Take a look at the team around you: who is missing from the mix?

What Luminaries do

So what do Luminaries consider to be work? To think and to think right... now that's real work to the Luminary. Some arrive at it by way of lots of reading, some by observation and meditation, some by interaction and questioning. (You do not have to have a college degree to be a Luminary.) There are many inputs, but the output is doing the work of thinking properly about life. His Australian competitor asked the Managing Director of a successful British company what he does every day when he closes his office door from 1 p.m. to 2 p.m. "I talk to my Creator about how he runs the universe." Caution: Luminary at work.

How would you respond to that statement? Do you think it is a good use of time? Here's how the other -EMONs may respond:

Entrepreneur	"That's all very well but while you are in there I am out pounding the pavement, doing deals and closing on opportunities."
Manager	"I believe that your Creator set some procedures and laws in place some time ago that work the same every day so that we can get on with our jobs. Until we get the notice that the sun will rise in the West or that gravity has been reversed, what's there to talk about?"
Organizer	"You have no idea about the number of jobs I take care of for you and the fires I put out—practical things—while you are in there thinking. Get a dose of reality... there are jobs to do."
Networker	"I know someone—my cousin's friend—who knows this Creator guy. Maybe we could all do lunch sometime. Anyway, there is this tremendous opportunity I came across when I was talking to Bob. It's a done deal really. All we have to do is all meet and ..."

Luminaries think for work. They wrestle with ideas, they dialogue, they form perspectives, and they often write them down. They think through the implications for communities and for their organization in particular. They then try to translate these into what they consider to be specific initiatives or instructions. (These are often not specific enough to be of any use to anyone else, but a Luminary doesn't always see this. If they get too specific they think they are insulting others by taking away the opportunity to do a bit of thinking of their own.) You can ask a Luminary, "What are you thinking about nowadays? What questions are you pondering? What about the current status quo are you questioning? What new insights are you gleaning, and what are your sources?" If you are a Luminary, you would welcome a dialogue sparked by these questions. If you are thinking, "Who on earth asks questions like this?" then, chances are, you are not a Luminary.

Luminaries don't just think, they also plan. These aren't necessarily the detailed, action plans of the Manager. They are the "big picture" plans which may include more adjectives than verbs. Because of the long-range nature of their plans, they may succeed slowly and, unfortunately, fail slowly.

At the heart level, Luminaries love, care, feel and experience emotion, but they often come to it by way of the mind. Others accuse them of living in their head, or not connecting their head and heart. This shows a lack of understanding about Luminaries. (One of the greatest insults we can level at a person—regardless of how they are wired—is that they do not love. What we are really saying is, "You do not love the way I want to be loved.") Luminaries love their fellow man not because they have the spontaneous passion of a Networker, but because it is the right thing to do, and in the end it is essential to making life work, and it is what life is all about. A "pure-ish" Luminary gets to this through rational deduction as they mature. Others may get there out of instinct, but not know why. Is one better than the other? That depends on which LEMON you are. I spoke with a friend who at 23 was a fully tenured professor at UC Berkeley. Through a long process of study and reasoning he had come to some decisions about spiritually. "I have two volumes written on the intersection of philosophy and religion," he told me "and another twelve volumes in my head." So I asked, "What are you going to do when those twelve volumes are complete?" He replied, "Love people. The end of it all is simply to love people." He is a fascinating person, but has been known to hibernate from people for seasons. He has arrived at the need to love by reasoning, not by primal urging.

Work takes place at three interconnected levels. To make it simple I have delineated these as the work of the head, the hands, and the heart. The table below summarizes a few things that the Luminary considers to be work at the Head, Hands and Heart level. You will find tables like this throughout the book to help synthesize your thinking and to help you build your Personal LEMON Profile using a chart in the Appendices.

Head	Hands	Heart
Think - wrestle with thoughts from all angles	Write - lots of theory	Ponder - ramifications of theories
Dialogue - listen for ideas that support and challenge those already brewing internally	Create space for solitude - necessary for making sense out of the bigger ideas	Wonder - about the ripple effects of their deeper thoughts
Question the "whys" of life	Plan big	Dream - about the transcendent value of such deep thinking
		Foster passion for their life ideas

How much Luminary do you have in your LEMON mix? Place a check mark in the appropriate column below, tally the marks in each column, then multiply the total by the factor indicated in each column. You can begin building your own LEMON Profile as you go along by transferring the grand total to the worksheet in the Appendix.

LEMON characteristics that I share	Not at all	Somewhat	A lot
1. Believe that ideas precede activities.			
2. Long range thinker.			
3. Inspire others through the power of ideas.			
4. Thought leader, valuing concepts and fresh thinking.			
5. Intuitively perceive where future lies.			
6. Sense future implications of today's thinking.			
7. Care more about the "Why."			

Now total your score	0	__x1	__x3

Luminary total	

Now transfer this total to the Luminary spot on the "Your LEMON Profile" worksheet in the Appendix.

Chapter 03
Entrepreneurs

*E*ntrepreneurs
move resources from areas of
low to high return. Ideas are a
dime a dozen. What matters is
turning them into results.

The word "entrepreneur" actually comes from the French who, at the time, referred rather disdainfully to Britain as a nation of shop-keepers. In the era of the landed gentry, being an Entrepreneur wasn't necessarily a badge of honor. But the same spirit that gave life to the Reformation in some European countries created the possibility of a groundswell of Entrepreneurs, people who felt they could seize opportunities and create their own destinies. I love the entrepreneurial spirit of many people I meet in Silicon Valley. It is fantastic to watch people find a legitimate need and then take a run at creating products and building companies that meet those needs.

My observation is that there are relatively more Entrepreneurs than Luminaries in the world. But not all the people who think that they are Entrepreneurs are actually wired as such. Almost 80% of college students say they want to be Entrepreneurs, and less than 40% actually start businesses. Why? We will find out more later. For the moment, let's look at some of the characteristics of Entrepreneurs.

Characteristics of Entrepreneurs

First, they believe that opportunities precede activities. (For the Luminary it was ideas that preceded activity.) An Entrepreneur can see opportunities where others see difficulties, challenges, opposition or... nothing. They are not starry-eyed about everything working out fine. Good Entrepreneurs sift out bad opportunities quickly. At the top venture capitalist firms a partner will see 1,500 plans a month and look closely at only five. They have an incredible knack of spotting good opportunities and people. One Entrepreneur I know told me he picks good people and then finds something for them to do. The opportunity for him is the person with promise. Human capital—and leadership in particular—is a precious asset.

Entrepreneurs are opportunists in the most positive sense of the word. Where a Luminary creates their own card game, Entrepreneurs make the most of whatever hand they are dealt. It's not their job to figure out whether this is the most well thought out card game in the world; it is their job to figure out how to win.

Don't think that Entrepreneurs don't create things: they can create organizations out of nothing. (Luminaries can create ideas out of nothing, but that doesn't always translate to building an organization that can deliver on those ideas.) Entrepreneurs have a great gift for accumulating the resources that are needed to make an entity viable, particularly during the early stages of the organization. Luminaries create intellectual capital; Entrepreneurs put together the right mix of intellectual, human, financial, spiritual and relational capital to make an entity work.

> "Innovation is the specific instrument of
> entrepreneurship... the act that endows resources
> with a new capacity to create wealth."
> (Peter Drucker, *Innovation and Entrepreneurship,* 1985)

The depth of field of an Entrepreneur is typically a lot shorter than that of the Luminary. To be successful they have to be able to focus on what is crucial now, because they know that tomorrow may not come if cash flow isn't there on Friday, an opportunity is not won this week, or a critical hire isn't made this month. Many Entrepreneurs are short-to-medium term thinkers. If they take too long-term a view, then they will dull their ability to separate the good from the bad. Remember, their stock-in-trade is opportunities, not ideas.

Where the Luminary inspires the organization through ideas, or exhausts the organization if they have too many, the Entrepreneur inspires the organization through their energy and enthusiasm. Working with them is like following in the slipstream of a NASCAR. Having committed to lead an organization, they will go at full speed to make it work.

You can tell quite a bit about leaders through their perception of and reaction to failure. Luminaries can see the destruction of their work as the elimination of lots of mistakes. Charles Franklin Kettering said, "An inventor fails 999 times, and if he succeeds once, he's in. He treats his failures simply as practice shots." Entrepreneurs don't fail, they just have learning experiences. If they are not failing at something then they are probably not pushing hard enough. They don't need to have the "one right thing" that must succeed at all costs. If something doesn't work then they will find another opportunity. They can tolerate risk and know that all ventures have some risk. The smart ones will try to minimize risk, but they will not try to avoid it all together. Entrepreneurs are, in fact, willing to alter the ideas of the Luminaries if that is what is necessary for the venture to succeed. They are not the protectors of the "uncompromising vision" of the Luminary because they figure that you may have to make some compromises here and there to make things succeed.

"As long as a person doesn't admit he is defeated,
he is not defeated - he's just a little behind and isn't
through fighting." (Darrell Royal)

Entrepreneurs win fast and fail fast, which in itself is not seen as a failure, provided it is fast. Slow failure… that's for the delusional Luminaries.

You can spot an Entrepreneur in part through what they value. They like people who start things and get things done. They value those who can spot a gap and find a way to fill it, usually profitably, whether a child with a lemonade stand, or a mother making muffins to put her kids through school, or a software engineer who turns business person. Entrepreneurs care more about results – the "Wherefore" – rather than the "Why."

What Entrepreneurs do

Entrepreneurs identify needs, find ways to fill needs, and then find ways to design, build, market and manage those products. The same is true in service organizations that have programs that are akin to the products of businesses. For those involved in the business world, successful Entrepreneurs build organizations in support of their products,

The Entrepreneur's definition of work therefore has many more verbs in it than does that of the Luminary. By nature Entrepreneurs are more pragmatic than Luminaries, although there are in fact abstract Entrepreneurs just as there are concrete Luminaries So let's look at the head, hands and heart of the Entrepreneur.

Head	Hands	Heart
Look for Opportunities Conduct focused research in support of or in search of a particular opportunity Keep their ears/eyes open Build organizations Anticipate and minimize risk… then move on in faith	Sell the new opportunity to those who can help bring it about—financiers, staff, customers, etc. Pull together the necessary elements for opportunity to happen (people, capital, space, etc.) Constantly make adjustments until something works, or until the writing is on the wall that it won't work	Embrace new opportunities with a passion Dwell on new angles Remain up-beat Overcome

How much Entrepreneur do you have in your LEMON mix? Place a check mark in the appropriate column below, tally the check marks in each column, then multiply the total by the factor indicated in each column. Add this to your own LEMON Profile by transferring the grand total to the worksheet in the Appendix.

LEMON characteristics that I share	Not at all	Somewhat	A lot
1. Believe that opportunities precede activities.		(	
2. Short-to-medium term thinker.		\	
3. Inspire others through energy and enthusiasm.			(
4. Will do any tasks in the early stages of venture.		(	
5. Can envision and create something out of nothing.			(
6. See "failure" as learning experience.		(	
7. Care more about results – the "wherefore."		(	
8. Value those who spot opportunities and take action to make them happen.		\	

Now total your score	0	__x1	__x3

Entrepreneur total	

Transfer this total to the Entrepreneur spot on the "Your LEMON Profile" worksheet in the Appendix.

Chapter 04
Managers

*J*ust tell me exactly what you want accomplished, then I will do everything to make it happen.

My colleagues and I had just run a consultation on LEMON Leadership with a group of executives. People were fired up with a new understanding of how they were wired as leaders. As a team my client recognized that in their recent history they had systematically chased off Luminaries and Entrepreneurs, and they talked about addressing the issue. They had a new way to dialogue together about leadership. The next morning, however, one of them raised his hand and with a serious look on his face said, "I have only one problem with your model. It should be called MELON leadership."

"Let me guess... you must be a Manager."
It is not that hard to spot Managers.

I tell this story because it contains another leadership truism that I have observed over and over.

LEMON TRUISM: Managers think that they are the plumb center of leadership, the only ones with a true grasp on reality, the truly sane ones at the party.

The M is in the middle because the Manager is the needle of the compass that is set to True North. In the eyes of the Manager, every other type of leader is some degree off center. In fact, next to them are the Entrepreneurs and the Organizers, and out in the fringes of leadership land are Luminaries and Networkers... way off center. That's the way Managers see the world. In my book, they are probably right on many counts.

If we have a me-centric view of leadership then Managers are the leaders that the other LE-ONs love to hate. We all know we need them, but we would rather not be like them. That's because we rather fancy ourselves as Indiana Jones and not as people who know how to make things and organizations work. We would rather be credited with breakthrough ideas than make people effective in their jobs. We would rather be a lion tamer than make sure that the lions are fed regularly.

Characteristics of Managers

A healthy Manager will concur that there needs to be fresh thinking and a proper identification of opportunities. But Managers believe that the real work has yet to start. To them, proper planning precedes activities. The game doesn't really begin until you have a game plan. Anything you do before you have the plan is probably just activity, not to be confused with work. Planning takes thought, energy, and discipline, This is not to say that it is bereft of intuition or that you cannot have intuitive Managers—of course you can—but they are intuitive about what needs to be set in place at a structural level to make things happen predictably, again and again. To the Manager, anyone can do something once, but it takes a certain amount of process and discipline to make something happen again and again at acceptable quality levels.

I was involved in a venture when a true blue Manager said, "Just tell me exactly what you want accomplished, then I will do everything to make it happen." I thought to myself, "If I tell him exactly what needs to be done, surely I will be insulting him. Shouldn't I leave a little room for him to do some creative guessing?" He was not insulted at all because he knew that my definition of "exactly what I wanted done" was a 20,000 foot version of what I wanted to see as an outcome, plus some broad guidelines as to process. He as a Manager would take it down to ground level and develop a concrete plan that would actually get it done. This interaction gives a sneak insight into the disconnects that can occur between the different leadership types. *

LEMON TRUISM: Great dreams have to be translated into concrete plans that are actionable by regular people before things actually happen.

You should seldom see a good Manager in a panic. Even an excitable, extroverted Manager is not prone to panic because they either think things through in advance or, if they haven't thought it all out, they use a trusted process that will deliver a sound result. Should everything fail, a Manager knows that they could not have saved the day with energy or ideas or networks—it was what it was. They are therefore the more levelheaded of the LEMON types.

Managers are deliberate. When dealt a hand they don't like, they systematically go about changing it until they have something that works. They won't reinvent the game. They will take the reality as it is and intentionally change it to something better over time. Once it is working, they leave it the way it is. My wife, Lyn, taught at an elementary school where the year's results rested on the final examination. Some people were shocked that the headmaster used the same examination papers year after year, simply collecting them from students when the exam was done and locking them in the safe until next year. "The only students who see them twice will be those who failed the year… and they are unlikely to remember them." He had a system that worked and did not want to waste teacher time and energy setting "original" examination papers every year. He was a Manager.

There is a common myth that "visionary" is a separate category of leadership. If this was true, the book would have been called VENOM Leadership… not a very attractive title. Every leadership type has vision, and the Managers are excellent implementers of vision, particularly that which requires more than just a short-term project to achieve good results. Managers have an understanding of what it takes to build an organization that will work effectively. As such, they would rather build a team to get the job done than do it themselves. This sounds trivial, but recognize that the tendency of Luminaries, Entrepreneurs and Organizers is to jump in the trench themselves and hope that through the sheer brilliance of the trench digging idea (L), or the raw enthusiasm for playing in mud (E), or the dedication to doing anything that is needed (O), others will soon rush to be in the trench, where the Networker is making sure everyone is having fun. It is interesting that during the course of writing this book we have seen two major catastrophes, namely, the tsunami in Southeast Asia, and Hurricane Katrina in the Gulf of Mexico. Here in the US it didn't take more than two days for people to start complaining that FEMA was not responding quickly enough. No matter how measured and reasoned the explanations of the FEMA leaders were about their plans and procedures, people wanted action, not plans. Their plan may have been fine, but people wanted immediate relief. This can be contrary to the deliberate workings of Managers.

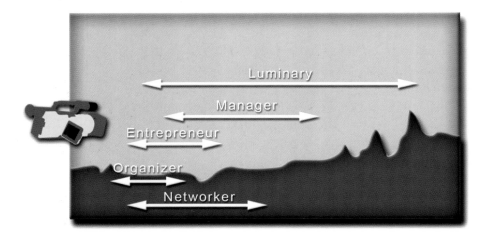

When looking at reality, each LEMON has a different focal length: different amounts are in clear view at any point in time. Managers are longer-term thinkers than Entrepreneurs, with a depth of focal length that is not as long as that of a Luminary, but longer than an Entrepreneur. They think in years more than decades; they are not panicked by what happens in a quarter if the outlook for the year is sound.

We have spoken of the Manager's penchant for planning. Another ability of note is their understanding of Process. To some people a process is a bureaucratic overlay or administrative burden that gets piled on top of a simple task to make it controllable by, well,

Managers. You can find control freaks in any of the LEMONs as this is a symptom of damage in the individual, and we are all damaged goods at some level. Damage leads to insecurity, and this can lead to control issues. True Managers know, however, that processes are there to free people to be the best they can be. Processes ensure that people know what to do, how to do it, and what constitutes a job well done precisely so that people can get on and do the job without having to continually check in with superiors to get directions. Good Managers have empty desks because they have planned for the right resources to do things and created processes that enable others to get them done. They find greater joy in building people and organizations than in simultaneously spinning an unmanageable number of plates.

Managers also understand profits. (Entrepreneurs and Networkers understand deals.) This does not mean that Managers are greedy and will only do things if there is money in it, but they are less inclined to do something on an emotional or ideological whim just because people are excited about it. Put another way, they have a realistic assessment of what things—particularly projects and new ventures—will really cost.

Finally, where Luminaries think about "Why" and Entrepreneurs think about "Wherefore", Managers think about "How"... and some might add, "How much."

What Managers do

The characteristics of Managers give a fair idea of what they consider to be real work. With each of the LEMONs believing that their work is central and the surrounding work of the other LEMONs is perfunctory, what is it that Managers see as the heart of work? Taking an idea or an opportunity (both of which are a dime a dozen, in their books) and turning it into a detailed plan is one of the things that a Manager regards as real work. While a Manager with a limited scope of work is able to recognize the boundaries of their work and stay within these lines, a senior executive who is a Manager is able to consider the end-to-end

Operating Model of the organization. (The book I-Operations gives an in-depth treatment of this subject.) Managers envision, design and implement processes that help people and companies get things done. They build teams that build systems that build products that meet needs of customers. Managers set up reporting mechanisms that keep everyone informed about whether the organization is on track. Work for them revolves around core business processes, not the fluff at the edges.

The Manager heart: some people mistakenly think this is an oxymoron. The Manager has a principled heart. This may not be the fiery, passionate heart of one of the other LE-ONs, but it is just as valid. A Manager develops a love for things and sticks to the commitments that love requires because it is right, not because it is easy or nice. I have watched Managers develop a following because their people know that the Manager actually cares for them, albeit with a Managerial kind of style. (The Networker makes you feel that you are their best friend in the world after just five minutes. The Manager may give some clues that you are a friend after five months… and a friend for life after five years.) Style can get in the way of a Manager, betraying their underlying heart. If a Manager is introverted, shy, cautious or plodding, others can perceive them as being heartless. Good Managers recognize this and make adjustments.

Managers get satisfaction from seeing things working well and people gainfully employed. A colleague once said, "Brett, I have never worked so hard in all my life!" Music to a Manager's ears. Underutilization of assets is not good news for Managers.

Reality Index

Take a look at the summary chart below and consider which of these activities describe you, or a Manager whom you know.

Head	Hands	Heart
Detailed planning Consider end-to-end models Envision processes to overcome obstacles	Build teams Implement details organization-wide Establish structures for reporting, communication and everything else Implement core business processes	Care for the improvement of people over the long-haul Delight in the efficiency of the organization Worry about chaos they aren't allowed to fix

Managers define reality

"This family is whacked!"

This was the pronouncement by our son, James, as he sat working on the computer one day with the rest of his family in the general proximity.

"What makes you say that?" I asked while doing my exercises by yanking on a rope and pulley contraption designed for astronauts.
"Well, there's my sister Fay, smiling in every photograph, but she's the most complex person I know. Then there's Davey and Mom…" At this point David was dressed in a half completed urchin outfit that Lyn was sewing for the school production of Oliver. He did look a bit unusual. "Then there's you on the rope…"
"So you think that you are the only normal one in the family, right?"
"Yes. That's right!"

James is a Manager. The left side of his brain scores a 97%. From his perspective he is absolutely convinced that what he sees is reality, and the rest of us are just a little unreal, to put it nicely.

My suspicion is that you have an intuitive sense of what I call "The Reality Index" of others. Someone presents something to you, you evaluate not just what they are saying, but you are looking for twitching eyebrows, conviction in their voice, steadiness of their gaze, tempered enthusiasm… you are creating their Reality Index. If you have known them for some time, you have already made a determination about how realistically they see things, and you apply a reality factor to what they are saying. You are dividing by 2, or multiplying by 1.3 to get to your assessment of reality. For Managers, 1 + 1 generally approximates 2. This is one of their strengths. It sounds simple, but remember that leaders define reality, so this gives Managers some advantages in leadership.

How much Manager do you have in your LEMON mix? Place a check mark in the appropriate column below, tally the check marks in each column, then multiply the total by the factor indicated in each column. You can begin building your own LEMON Profile as you go along by transferring the grand total to the worksheet in the Appendix.

LEMON characteristics that I share	Not at all	Somewhat	A lot
1. Believe that proper planning precedes activities.		X	
2. Long term thinker.		X	
3. Inspire others through ability to execute.			X
4. Will build teams to get things done rather than do it themselves.			X
5. Will deliberately reshape a situation until it becomes viable.	X		
6. Understands process, policies, planning and profits – the "how."		X	

Now total your score	0	_3_ x1	_2_ x3

Manager total			9

Methodically transfer this total to the Manager spot on the "Your LEMON Profile" worksheet in the Appendix.

Chapter 05
Organizers

*O*rganizers are an under-recognized corps of people who don't fit into the traditional management and leadership molds, yet they are essential to the healthy functioning of any group.

Many corporations make the mistake of overlooking Organizers when considering people for senior leadership positions because, unless they have a very strong secondary DNA strand, they are hard to categorize. They simply don't do things in the traditional way, so they are disregarded. Once you have come to know Organizers, however, they become easy to recognize, and they can be called out to take up their full role in an organization.

I owe a special debt to Organizers. There is something hidden in every community that keeps things working. There is oil that keeps the more glorious parts of the organization from getting stuck. There is an unconscious work that removes the obstacles to everyday living, and much of this is done by under-appreciated Organizers. I am grateful for this particular type of leader and how they have made my life more livable.

LEMON TRUISM: Leaders are designed to be in teams where all five slices of the lemon are active and honored.

Before I describe the characteristics of Organizers let me expand on this leadership truism. First, leaders are meant to function in teams. Unfortunately we celebrate the individual, from the President to the Most Valuable Player. But solo leadership is seldom effective. Second, who heads the leadership team should be more a matter of influence, ability and gravitas and less a matter of hierarchical position. Too often we appoint a leader to fill a vacuum "at the top," and this gives permission to others to be second tier players. Third, the most effective teams are those where all fives slices of the LEMON are present, and where the stated team leader yields to the gifting of the particular leader needed in a specific situation. Where the leader is an Organizer it is particularly important that these constructs be in place, and we will come to see why when we explore the characteristics of an Organizer.

Organizers like to have all their equipment with them. They know the minimum set of tools needed to get things done, and they don't count on others to show up at the right time with the right tools. Organizers are not necessarily gifted to anticipate well in advance what should be done; they don't lay out the best plans; but they do anticipate that something will go wrong, and they are there with the toolbox to remedy things.

Characteristics of Organizers

First, let's lay aside the myth that Organizers are organized in the traditional sense of the word. They seldom are. Don't be thrown off the trail if they don't have tidy desks, neat closets and clean cars. While Organizers can indeed be neatniks, being organized is not a prerequisite for being an Organizer. Being organized implies having a system and routine that gets followed with some predictability. Few of the Organizers I have met are like this. Why? Because Organizers are highly intuitive problem solvers. They are fire fighters, and one can seldom predict where fires will break out. What you can predict is that shortly after they do, an Organizer will be on the scene.

Unconscious Competence   **Conscious Competence**

Organizers are very capable people who function with a high degree of instinct. They are often looked down on because they cannot explain why or how they do things, but they have a better sense than most about what it takes to actually get things done. In the competencies continuum you can safely say that they have an unconscious competence. An Organizer is not the person who will write the procedures manual because, in their minds, they just do things that are obvious to them. They often put themselves down because they don't have the formal structure and packaging of the other leaders, and therefore feel that they have very little to teach others.

This is not to say that Organizers don't have systems. They certainly do, but unless they have a dose of Manager in them, the Organizers cannot explain their systems to others in a way that sounds plausible. Their high dose of instinct makes them suspicious of the systems of others for reasons they cannot articulate, but often because they believe that they have a faster track to completion.

Organizers have the ability to prioritize on the urgent. You may be saying, "Don't confuse the urgent with the important." Let's acknowledge that there are times when the urgent is indeed important, and give Organizers their due. They can intuitively pick the right things to focus on at any point in time.

Can an Organizer be a CEO?

I have never met Neutron Jack Welch, the past CEO of General Electric. I watched footage of his transition to leadership decades ago, and have observed him from a distance. He will go down in history as one of the more effective GE CEOs. In my view, he is an Organizer-Entrepreneur. Few frills, little regard for corporate politics and convention, and an intense focus on near term results.

One of the frustrations faced by Organizers is losing the long term thread. It is therefore important to the sanity of an Organizer that they see a series of short-term gains. Holding out for the prize that comes after three years and nine months doesn't cut it for them. When working with Organizers make sure that you don't lock them into the long-term picture so much that they cannot experience some victory this week. One of my personal wishes is that I had become a student of my wife, Lyn, a lot sooner. Had this been the case I would have recognized her need for weekly victories, and not just 5 year plans. This is a legitimate Organizer-need, so the wise leader creates a composite of the immediate and the long term. Organizers likewise have a responsibility to set their daily To Do List in the context of the longer term picture of fellow LEMONs.

This brings me to the next thing about Organizers that makes them easy to identify: they love to "bring things to a close." I sat in a brainstorming meeting with an Organizer—this was the stated purpose of the meeting to explore how to approach a LEMON Leadership Forum—and five minutes into it she had scooted her chair away from the conference table and was at her desk typing. "What are you doing?" I asked, abandoned at the brainstorming table. "The brochure," she answered. She had scanned the conversation for an action item (even though we hadn't decided to proceed with the event), deduced there was something she could bring to a close, and headed off to just do it.

Organizers, like the other LEMONs, have a different definition of words like "done" and "completed" and "finished." We moved offices once while I was out of town. In two days it was "done," and then I noticed that the cubes were not exactly connected to the walls... plus a few other details. So I waited for the people in charge (who were Organizers) to finish the job. Silly me. I then learned that in their book, it was done. I would have been smarter to have a Manager draw up the move plan, have Organizers get the lion's share of the work done, then have the Manager dog down the details until it was 98% done and then ignore the other 2%. Seventy percent. I work with an Organizer who hates it when I say that number, but my rule of thumb is that Organizers are done at about 70% complete. So if you are a Luminary, Entrepreneur or Manager and an Organizer says something is done, it may be that it is not quite done in your books.

For the Organizer the quick result is the best result... usually always. Tie this back to the penchant for action, bringing things to a close, and the 70% solution, and you can see why this is true. Sooner is better than later. They would rather take a chance that something is wrong and re-do it later than see it lying around open-ended for a long time. Unresolved things—whether tasks or relationships—are an Organizer's worst nightmare. Incomplete tasks create tension. I have 3,000+ emails in my inbox, most of which are read. I scan them for action items, memory joggers, and trails of open conversations. Lyn only keeps the unread items that require action on her screen, and she gets agitated it they fill more than one page.

A final characterisitic of Organizers is that they care about "When." Not "Why," "Wherefore," "How"... but the "What/When" combination. (And the "When" for them is usually immediately.)

What Organizers do for work

It is fun to see Organizers at work as they fly into action and focus with intensity on getting something closed out. They keep a mental catalogue of loose ends (some may actually have lists in writing) and efficiently discern the critical path to closure. They quickly figure out what the issues are, and who has them. These aren't just task related issues, because the Organizer is highly perceptive about the People issues: who is on board, who has authority, who is at odds with others, who is happy and unhappy. Organizers are right up with Networkers in being attuned to the matters of contentment, dissension and the mood of people. (Networkers want people to be happy with them: Organizers want people to be happy in their own right, but also because their lack of contentment will kill getting the job done. Quickly.)

So having done the work of finding the issues (not via a committee meeting or astute analysis, like the Manager, but by instinct), the Organizer creates on-the-spot solutions that may not be sustainable over time, but are good enough for now.

> **LEMON TRUISM: Leaders have a perpetual responsibility to renew the Operating Model of the organization.**

Managers are better at creating process than Organizers, but they don't always know when the process has joined the walking dead. An Organizer knows when a process has to be refreshed, when it no longer has life. They can tell when something isn't working, no matter how good it looks on paper. In fact, the phrase "this isn't working" is often a telltale sign that you are dealing with an Organizer.

Where there is growth, progress, development or "life," there will always be the need to have some aspect of the Operating Model under construction. Managers want things nailed down and left alone, so their greatest ally can be an Organizer who has a nose for when things are getting stale, provided the Manager fights the natural tendency to view the Organizer as a renegade.

Organizers work to defend the needy. I am not sure if this is because their function has historically been overlooked by leadership theorists and because they as people are often taken for granted or marginalized, but Organizers have the ability to empathize with those in need, and they take on the practical concerns of those who are less empowered than others. This is a great asset to any corporation and the community it serves. By the same token, Organizers need to beware that they can quickly point out the faults of those "who should know better" (their LEM-N colleagues) for failing to continuously meet the needs of people whom they are leading. The very fact that Organizers cast themselves as under-the-radar folks gives them permission (in their own logic, albeit faulty) to criticize those who more readily don the leadership mantle.

Head	Hands	Heart
Figure out the shortest route to closure	Act by instinct now; think later	Sense
		Intuit
Find out what the issues are, and who has them	Get the job done	Experience the satisfaction of a job done
	Resolve issues	
Create on-the-spot solutions	Reduce stress	Defend the needy
	Keep the process fresh	

If the organization were a body

Analogies are usually incomplete, but a final way to understand Organizers is to think of the organization as a body, and you might say:

- The Luminary may be the brain.
- The Entrepreneur could be the heart and muscle.
- The Manager could be seen as the skeleton.
- The Networker is the nervous system, transmitting communications.
- The Organizer could be seen as the blood going back and forth through the body, cleaning up the junk, attacking intruders, spotting where things are dead, and bringing fresh life and energy where needed.

One more tip in spotting Organizers: when someone says to me, "I don't care what my title is or what my position is in the hierarchy…" it is a good clue that they are an Organizer. They are genuine when they say this, not falsely modest. Another of the LEMONs may feel they need the title to get a job done; an Organizer feels that what they need is space, free reign, and for people and formal processes to get out of their way.

How much Organizer do you have in your LEMON mix? Place a check mark in the appropriate column below, tally them in each column, then multiply the total by the factor indicated in each column.

LEMON characteristics that I share	Not at all	Somewhat	A lot
1. Action oriented.			X
2. Have an unconscious competence and an intuitive ability to pick the right thing to focus on.		X	
3. Love to bring things "to a close."	X		
4. Will do any tasks to get a quick result.	X		
5. Good at identifying issues.		X	
6. Practical and quickly get to what needs to be done without much planning.		X	
7. Care more about closure – the "when."	X		

Now total your score	0	_2_ x1	_1_ x3

Organizer total	6

Quickly transfer this total to the Organizer spot on the "Your LEMON Profile" worksheet in the Appendix.

Chapter 06
Networkers

*N*etworkers are the fifth essential leadership type—essential in the sense that they are a critical component of the makeup of any organization.

The challenge for Networkers is that they are often viewed as the hail-fellow-well-met glad hands of the corporation who are not serious leaders. They make the party fun, they add some warmth to the fire, they help people feel good, but they are not real executive material. Nothing could be further from the truth. There are seasons that call for a Networker. At a time when Cisco needed to go on an acquisition spree to fill out its product portfolio, who better to have at the helm than a Networker?

LEMON TRUISM: Different leaders are better suited to different stages of the corporate lifecycle, but this does not mean it is best to replace the leader as the corporation progresses through its stages.

Leaders must be coached to grow with the organization. The maturing of people takes them on a journey from a "me" to an "us" view of life. Likewise, a maturing leader will determine how others on the leadership team must augment their type of leadership. Once you have determined your primary and secondary leadership type, you then need to plot a growth path for yourself. Corporations will increasingly be architected to look like the organic organisms they have become thanks to the enabling technology of the Internet. Hierarchical and formal corporations will decrease. The ecosystem of an organization will become as important as its own identity as it seeks to have impact. Therefore we will need more Networkers in leadership circles. This is no less true in the personal realm. The horizontal spreading of information among people, including children, puts everyone on a more equal playing field. This is not to say that there should not be traditional roles such as parents and children, but it is to say that the way in which we interact with our children or parents will be, at some levels, more peer-to-peer than in the past. Networker DNA is well suited to this scenario.

Characteristics of Networkers

Networkers are often the most likeable of the LEMONs. They have an ability to connect with people and draw them into their relational orbit quickly and warmly. When you consider your Networker friends there is usually a smile on your face while you think of them. Networkers have an uncommon grace for relationships. Somehow people cut them relational slack even if they fail to meet expectations. I have many Networker friends who, despite the faults that all of us have, are still liked and likeable. There are mean-spirited Networkers, to be sure, but it is harder for them to stay this way because it works against their identity. Liking and being liked are part of their fingerprint.

> **LEMON TRUISM: We live in an increasingly networked world where the organizing principle for organizations will similarly be the network.**

Networkers love to bring people together. At the corporate level, when it comes to the modus operandi for getting things done, Networkers have a belief that work starts by gathering a group—not with idea formulation or planning. One of the common beliefs of Networkers is this: "If we get enough smart people in the room, the right thing is sure to happen." This statement encapsulates many of the plusses and minuses of Networkers. A year or so ago I participated in a large gathering organized—and I use the term loosely—by a Networker whose assistant, unhappily, was also a Networker. In the build up to the conference I began to notice the Networker patterns: excellent speakers were gathered, themes were waved back and forth, possibilities for the agenda were floated as trial balloons, connections were made. By the time I got to the meeting I had decided to hang loose—this meeting might be effective, but it would not be structured. Things were clearly going to happen more by relational osmosis than design. There was no sense in pressing for clarity, and a lot of reason to go with the flow and try to serve the Networker in small ways that did not include adding too much structure. When I got to my breakout session where three businesspeople were to be "subject matter experts" it turned out that the local facilitator did not arrive. So, unfazed, I stepped in for that session. The facilitator never did arrive... no explanation was ever given, but then again, I didn't expect one. There is a saying, "love expects the best," but the problem is that we impose our definition of "best" on people whose best is not the same as ours. Imposing a Manager's view of Best Practices on an Organizer or Networker is not love.

Networkers are people oriented in a way that makes it easy for others to connect with them. They make people feel special, and are usually good at verbal affirmation. When a Networker sees you doing something well, she will assume that you always do that well, and that you similarly do other things well. Where the Manager is thinking, "Anyone can do something once" the Networker is saying, "You are always good at this!" Networkers are not only good at giving affirmation, but they like to receive it from others. Their love language is often words of affirmation. My wife, Lyn, is very good at verbal affirmation. She points out that we can remember the positive and negative comments made by teachers, parents, coaches, and friends long into our adult life. Not everyone in our family is good at verbal affirmation: Fay is better at writing cards, James at physical touch and, when pressured, writing a speechlett. Davey is naturally affirming and readily complements Lyn on what she is wearing or something she is doing. We all have to coach each other, and the Networker coaches us in verbal affirmation.

Networkers can find points of common ground as the basis for beginning things. In a conversation in the grocery line they will find the things they have in common with the Hungarian butterfly collector standing in front of them. "I see you drink milk...." Networkers will find a basis for building a bridge, and get to work on it quickly.

Not everyone does this; not everyone looks for points of commonality. A Luminary, for example, may look for points of idea conflict. Be cautioned, however, not to take the enthusiasm and verbal affirmation of the Networker as being actual agreement. They can say, "Yes, yes!" while not saying, "...but there are some points where I differ, and we can maybe work that out later."

Networkers have the ability to connect the dots on relationships that seem spurious to the rest of the LEMONs. They are not always right, but they believe in the power of relational networks, and they instinctively build people webs. When I go to conferences with lots of new people, I do best when I have a Networker with me. Without receiving any instructions, the Networker will come to me with a continual string of people that I "just have to meet." Even if I am not sure that the Networker has read it correctly, I usually follow their instincts.

Where Luminaries know intellectual capital and Entrepreneurs know financial capital and Managers know human capital, Networkers are experts at "relational capital." In fact, relationships are their stock in trade. They know that without a strong web of stakeholders, the best ideas and the hottest opportunities will amount to nothing.

Perhaps counter to what one would think, my observation is that Networkers are not really people driven, but "event driven." Where Luminaries are idea driven and Entrepreneurs are opportunity driven, for Networkers life revolves more around a series of events that inevitably involve people. This is what sparks them into action. They will build meetings and conferences and gatherings into their calendar because that is where things happen for them. Their choice of events will usually follow a theme that pertains to their work: trade shows, news conferences, client meetings. They have an instinct for showing up at the right places at the right time. Conferences are a place to remain connected—or be able to tell others that they are connected—to large groups of people at once.

"Bill and I were chatting the other day, Clinton, that is, and he shared with me..."

(The unimaginative Manager might have said, "I was attending a conference last week where Clinton was a keynote speaker, and he told the attendees...")

Let me build on this non-intuitive aspect of Networkers not being people driven. When it comes to when and why they communicate, even their communications are event-driven. They do not have the more deliberate communications of the other LEMO-s. This is not to say that they are not engaged when communicating one on one; they do this better than many others. But we will find out about the radar of Networkers in due course, and this will shed light on their event-driven communications.

Finally, Networkers care about "Who," or more specifically, who can help me accomplish my agenda at the moment, or who can I help achieve their dreams. Who are the players, who are the underdogs, who are the impacted ones, who are the ones I can impact?

What Networkers do for work

It takes real work to build a network. It takes persistence to forge the relational capital needed to have critical mass behind something. It takes real skills to intuit which people are helpful, and which groups may be detrimental to a venture. The work of Networkers revolves around this very task of networking. They determine which organizations and people should be connected to accomplish some purpose, and they are able to pencil the dots between such groups before others see the advantages of linkages. Their primary work therefore involves getting out there, meeting people, assessing what network they need to be successful, building that network one node at a time, and pulling the relational pieces together.

If you are a Manager right about now you are saying, "That's not real work! What about the business plans, the reports, the actual work of making stuff?" You are right to a degree: networks of people are fickle. They may not stand the test of time; they are not as predictable as your processes. But to a Networker plans and procedures are just details that people like you take care of. They are not the hard part, the real work, the fun part. Your work is just rote drudgery to the Networker. Life to the Networker is not about widgets, it is about people, connections... all the warm and fuzzy stuff.

Let's say that you are a Manager and you have taken a job as a sales person. There is no doubt that you could logically determine what needs to be done, plan your day, and execute the script. You could adapt your modus operandi to include the things on the work list of Networkers in the table below. But for you these things would be items you have to get done in order to get your real work achieved, namely taking orders, getting goods to customers, and meeting quota. To you they are check marks in the sales process because you know you have to play the game a certain way to win.

To the Networker this is the real work: relating to people, getting groups together, schmoozing, rubbing shoulders, touching base, checking in, conferencing, calling, doing life together... this is the work. Meeting quota is incidental. Life is about people and all the stuff that goes with them.

Head	Hands	Heart
Connect the dots	Relate	Desire the best for the people of the whole world
Consider the right people for the right things	Get groups together	Believe "it all comes down to people"
Think about who can fill holes in their network	Rub shoulders	
	Schmooze	Embrace new people
	Conference call	Downplay the negative, bad news
	Just get together and "do life"	

What business are you really in?

Know what your business is really all about. Every business has a simple cycle of Designing, Developing, Marketing and Managing products or services. This is true for a manufacturer and a charity. This does not automatically mean that every business is a product business. My wife, Lyn, has worked in direct sales for many years and leads a team of around 2,000 people. For more than 15 years she has noticed that the leaders who do well know that it is not a product business but a people business. If people are being grown and they are happy, then the leaders are happy. If they are not helping their people experience success, then they do not like their jobs. The products are incidental. It doesn't matter what the corporate brochure says, know the real nature of your business and adapt your work patterns accordingly. Networkers understand this better than most.

LEMON TRUISM: Know what business you are in and adjust how you do your LEMON work accordingly.

How much Networker do you have in your LEMON mix? Place a check mark in the appropriate column below, tally the check marks in each column, then multiply the total by the factor indicated in each column. You can begin building your own LEMON Profile as you go along by transferring the grand total to the worksheet in the Appendix.

LEMON characteristics that I share	Not at all	Somewhat	A lot
1. People aware; attuned to their stories.			
2. Love to bring people together.			
3. Instinctively build networks.			
4. Aware of relational capital.			
5. Know what people want or need.			
6. Understand that the "soft side" of things is really the hard side.			
7. Care more about connecting – the "who."			

	Not at all	Somewhat	A lot
Now total your score	0	__x1	__x3

Networker total	

Now weave this total into the Networker spot on the "Your LEMON Profile" worksheet in the Appendix.

Chapter 07
Lemon Squeeze

What **LEMONS**
protect under pressure

*Y*ou may have looked long and hard at the characteristics of LEMONs described in the earlier chapters and still be unsure of how you are wired. Don't give up.

There is another way to approach the discovery and that is to look closely at what leaders protect. The theory of LEMON Leadership is that different types of leaders will, by default, protect different things. They will also be less than protective about —as in willing to sacrifice—things that they do not deem to be important. I remember spending lots of time thinking about a topic, writing a paper, and polishing the constructs. I had ownership of it. I showed it to a Networker friend who felt quite comfortable saying "it was actually all of our thinking" and "why not put a few other names down as the authors." The Luminary in me reacted. When I sent the article off to a person he knew, the Networker in him reacted. I protected my article; he protected his network.

Before we dig into what LEMONs protect, remember that when things are going well the true wiring of a leader can be masked by a warm personality, easygoing ways, and camaraderie. In fact, some leaders do not discover that they have a second slice to their leadership until they get into a tough climate. A Networker may be the right CEO during an upward business cycle, but if she fails to discover her supplementary LEMON slices, she will not have the resources to cope during a down cycle.

In difficult times when tough choices have to be made, you can see quite clearly what it is that a leader protects. This will tell you much about who they are.

> Luminaries protect their ideas. They would rather lose the publisher than change the score, jeopardize the client than change the architecture, forego market share than compromise the design. They would rather die than compromise their view of the truth.

> Entrepreneurs protect opportunities. They will nurture an opportunity until it grows to have a life of its own. Until then they will protect it from the burdens of administrivia and the prying eyes of competitors and the other risks of its early life.

Managers protect policies, procedures, processes and established practices. Before you write them off as boring, realize that they have worked hard to figure out efficient and effective ways of getting things done so they are not about to let every new employee come along and meddle with the way things are done. They know how things work, and they protect the mechanisms that keep things working smoothly.

Organizers are a little more complex. When things are going well they are loyal to a key leader that they support (if they are not the #1 person in the organization) and they see themselves as the protector of that leader, often shielding them from many day-to-day annoyances. Should things, in their view, go wrong, then the Organizers protect themselves.

Networkers protect their network … their Rolodex, their web of relationships. Let's look at this more closely.

Giving away the crown

If you have traveled much you will know that different cultures hold things in relative regard. Truth, trust, being on time, privacy… these are some examples of cultural differences. When I go to Chile or China I need to know what their culture values highly. Interacting with LEMONs is like a cross-cultural experience in that the differences can be just as profound. The danger is that we are not attuned to them because we think we come from the same place.

In their unrefined state, each of the LEMONs will trade with the assets of the other LEMONs in a way that may horrify the one whose assets are being pawned. When we do not honor and respect and regard the other slices as being equally important to our own, then the perverse permutations of our behavior are many… too many to list here, but some examples follow.

Luminaries will churn through Entrepreneurs, spitting out those who don't totally align with and give expression to their ideas. They will set themselves above the corporate policies of the Managers, and ignore the issues raised by Organizers, or under-appreciate their work. They will see the relationships of Networkers as kindling to keep their ideas burning.

Entrepreneurs will play fast and loose with the ideas, designs, or constructs of Luminaries. They will circumvent the corporate processes of Managers, see Organizers as Peons, and use people as opportunity fodder rather than build relationship with them.

Managers will constrain the free thinking of Luminaries, trim the wings of Entrepreneurs, disdain the lack of structure of the more intuitive Organizers, and see the Networkers as flakes, thereby dishonoring their relationships.

Organizers will put more store on having short term aspects of the company work than in holding true to its purpose as articulated by the Luminary. They will compromise the opportunities of Entrepreneurs by going for quick answers, will yawn at the boring Managers, ignoring their procedures and finding ways to get around them to meet their own needs. They will favor their own intuition in relationships over the structured approaches to relationships that the Networkers have crafted.

Networkers will claim the ideas of Luminaries as their own. They will affix their names to other people's work, using the "we" word as their defense. They will lose opportunities rather than face conflict in a relationship. They will pooh-pooh the corporate processes of Managers (even if they are subconsciously fastidious about their own relational processes), and see the Organizers as replaceable worker bees.

Cutting the baby in half

The proverbially wise King Solomon figured out who was the real mother of a child by suggesting that the two "I-say-it's-mine" mothers cut the baby in two and each take a half. The real mother refused.

- If you are happy to cut a truth in two in order to promote your agenda, you are not a Luminary.
- If you are happy to kill a great opportunity in order to keep your view of the organization stable, you are not an Entrepreneur.
- If you are happy to short-circuit agreed upon policies, processes and methods in order to make something happen, you are probably not a Manager.
- If you don't care about the practical issues and details that it takes to actually make something happen (so long as the idea is good, the opportunity is great or the relationship has promise) you are not an Organizer.
- If you think that relationships with people, clients, suppliers and customers are boiler fuel, an easily replaced commodity, you are probably not a Networker.

Every day initiatives get killed in corporations simply because a decision maker concludes, "This is not my thing. It is not important to me." Yet many of those initiatives are exactly what the organization needs to be healthy and effective. The truth is that the leader who killed the initiative was reacting based on their identity instead of responding out of a complete view of healthy leadership. Next time think twice before you happily cut someone else's baby in half. The higher one climbs the ladder, the more rungs there are marked "ego" and the harder it is to separate things driven by our personal identity versus the true needs of the organization.

LEMON TRUISM: The slice that gave strength to the organization at its outset can be the cause of its downfall if it is used as an excuse for not adding other LEMON slices.

Think about this; it is a strong warning to not be blinded by our wiring to the preclusion of others and the truth they embody. How many organizations do you know that have so subscribed to their strength that it has become a weakness after 10 or 20 years?

I protect my…	Ideas	Opport-unities	Systems	Freedom to act	Rolodex

With your corporate back to the wall

The truisms about what we protect can be seen in the DNA of whole corporations too. Observe the companies you know well and you may see that their strong suit is coupled with what they protect and this in turn can negate other influences that could round out their DNA. Think through the table below and consider your own examples of where LEMON Leadership colors a company as a whole.

Corporate Strength	The organization protects:	And is resistant to:
Creating innovative products	Intellectual property	Outside ideas, and suffer from the NIH (not invented here) syndrome
Rapidly responding to opportunities	Agility	Formality in infrastructure and suffer from overdone chaos

Corporate Strength	The organization protects:	And is resistant to:
Building solid operations	The Business Plan, in all its glory	Anything fresh that would raise the "we don't have a scenario for this" flag
Dealing with crises	Independence	Anything that would codify the intuitive
Forming cross-corporation ecosystems	The right to relate broadly to many corporations	Measurement of the effectiveness of its relationships

This is true—if not truer—for non-profit corporations such as religious organizations or charitable groups. Here money is less of the driver, and the cause is often stronger. They are therefore all the more prone to the blindness that comes from the compelling cause, a blindness that obscures the perspectives of anyone who does not fit into the corporate mold, anyone who runs counter to the sub-culture. I recently observed the thinking patterns of a leader in a prominent denomination who sized up situations by taking his template of "what worked" and projecting it on situations with which he came in contact. This mental overlaying was used to suggest improvements which sounded like, "if they did it our way..." – strength had become the default template, and therefore a weakness.

We need five-slice leaders, and we need five-slice corporations. Resistance to who we are not leads to crippling bondage, individually and corporately. Ignorance about who we are has the same effect and inevitably results in us driving off, if not killing off, those who are not quite like us. Celebrate your strengths, and be careful what you protect.

I respond to pressure like a ...	L	E	M	O	N

Chapter 08
On a good day

LEMON
strengths

*K*nowing who you are as a leader will prevent you getting caught in the extreme fringes of life. One day you feel like Supermom, the next you feel like a sloth.

On a good day you are a capable leader looked to by many, the next day you are a culprit. One day you are on top of your game, the next you are a miserable spectator in the amphitheater of life. These are extremes, and knowing how we are wired will save us from arrogance on the one hand, or abject misery on the other. We are encouraged by ancient authors to have a healthy assessment of who we are. This chapter will help underline your strengths.

One more reminder about strengths and weaknesses before we get to the details for each of the LEMONs: an effective leader is a whole person in three connected areas - Head, Hands and Heart. These three elements of the leader's life cannot be separated. An effective leader is an integrated person who has no problem giving weight to the mind, the activities and the feelings simultaneously. We will therefore look at the intellectual, practical and emotional strengths, (or Head, Hands and Heart strengths) for each leader.

We can spot those who tilt towards one direction. A friend recently said, "I am having trouble thinking what I should be feeling." A head man. Or the bumper sticker I read today which stereotyped a situation: "You don't pray in my school and I won't think in your church." We will examine strengths in all three categories: head, hands, and heart.

Luminaries: Seeing the future

Luminaries see a future before it happens. They possess a knack for intuiting about how things are going to turn out even though they do not know all of the specifics. In most cases they don't really care too much about the "How" because they are convinced so much by the "Why" that they assume that the "How" will take care of itself. If you find this strange you are probably not a Luminary. Luminaries don't automatically have a high IQ. It is not about intelligence as much as how they see the world, a way of looking at life.

More specifically, it's about how they see the world working. Luminaries have an interest in dialoguing and an ability to understand the assumptions and worldview behind things, thereby "predicting" things that will fail and things that will succeed. They can spend a short amount of time evaluating an idea and spot whether there are faulty assumptions. They can spend a week in a country and piece together trends and national thought patterns and presuppositions that cannot be read in a book. Then years later they see them in a headline or a research paper.

In addition to seeing things clearly, many Luminaries can articulate them clearly, provided that they push through to the "simplicity on the other side of complexity." (To some Luminaries, however, things are so clear that they cannot understand how others could possibly struggle with the concepts, so they are unable to explain them clearly. This is more the exception than the rule.) A seasoned Luminary has gone beyond the fascination of complex arguments and can echo the saying, "The simple strive to be profound; the profound strive to be clear." Why? Because they believe that ideas have consequences and see themselves as incubators of ideas, baton carriers of truths. Remember, Luminaries protect ideas.

Passion can be a matter of temperament, culture or upbringing, and one cannot point to the presence or absence of passion as an indicator of whether one is a Luminary, or any of the LEMONs, for that matter. But when you scratch around, push and poke a little, you will find the Luminary's eyes light up around ideas. Luminaries get passionate about concepts and even methodologies. A friend recently mentioned he had examined 162 methodologies for strategic planning before choosing one, because "the one that I choose will have profound impacts on me six or seven years from now." Many Luminaries have the ability to blend principle and passion. They may not have passion for its own sake, but they are passionate about principles. They are like the architect of a skyscraper who was called in to examine the cracks that were developing on the 52nd floor. When entering the building he went to the basement and walked around until he discovered that a night watchman had been removing bricks one by one for a garage he was building at home. Luminaries examine foundational principles, bedrock constructs, rather than cracks in more obvious places.

Like Entrepreneurs, Luminaries can envision new products, systems and projects–even new societies. They can see something where there is nothing. They can see a patch of land and envision a Disneyland, take sand and air-conditioning (and loose laws) and envision a Las Vegas. They can see a product where others see the impossible. They can stay the course until things come to fruition because they believe that the right ideas produce the right results. Luminaries can suspend the pragmatic until the truth of an idea bears fruit.

Luminaries can be interested in many things with a fascination for areas beyond one specific domain. Recognizing that they possess certain thinking skills, they apply those same thinking skills to many areas. While not all Luminaries are multi-dimensional, those who are get referred to as "Renaissance People" because of their practical mastery of many topics. A trip to George Washington's home and how he innovated across many fronts gives the impression that he was such a man.

> **LEMON TRUISM: On a good day we operate from the Strengths of our primary LEMON type.**

Anything you can do…

Luminaries often have practical skills or talents across multiple areas. When you find them in corporations they are able to do things better than many others. They have no problem getting into the details of projects, quickly immersing themselves in the facts, but their involvement is for a different reason than that of the other LEMONs. They do it to move the idea forward, to help it along, or to speed the journey of the big idea. They do not do it because they relish the task as a long-term job.

There are exceptions to all of these observations, one of which would be the professorial type Luminary who is highly intelligent and highly detached from everyday tasks. Hand strengths are then limited to the things that need to be done in their particular field of study.

Principled passion

When it comes to the heart, Luminaries quickly embrace people who have a passion for the same ideas or causes. A walk through Oxford will take you to the Eagle and Child pub in Oxford's magnificent St. Giles thoroughfare where C.S. Lewis, Tolkien and others known as "The Inklings" had conversation that flowed quicker than warm beer. In intellectual settings Luminaries congregate like Oxford Dons to dialogue, sharpen each other's thinking, and warm each other's hearts in the process. Their mind filters out the misaligned people; their heart embraces those who are on the same mental bus. They are less sensitive to whether they actually like people, and more in tune with whether people like their ideas. They are happy to embrace all sorts of people and have less intuition than Networkers and Entrepreneurs about whether people are a good fit in a broad way. If they fit ideologically, then they generally are a fit for a Luminary. The corollary is that they can reject a good friend who simply differs on a point or two.

There are melancholic Luminaries, to be sure, but Luminaries as a group can stay focused on and upbeat about a dream, holding it in their hearts on a sustained basis. This means that they are less prone to ups and downs provided they stay focused on the main idea, and provided they have the basic disciplines to take small steps each day towards the fulfillment of the idea.

Entrepreneurs: Opportune risk

If Luminaries can sense the veracity of ideas, Entrepreneurs can intuitively sense the viability of opportunities. For them, opportunities are the main thing, not ideas. In fact, I have seen many entrepreneurs who are willing to sacrifice the "purity" of a Luminary's idea if it helps them realize the opportunity. In a sales process, for example, an architect or a professor would rather walk away than change something they believe is right. For the Entrepreneur, they will change things if it means securing the deal. Why? Don't they care about the principles? Not as much. They care about actually getting things to work, and if one has to sacrifice an idea or two along the road, so be it.

Entrepreneurs have a high tolerance for risk; they are not afraid of failure. Good entrepreneurs will correctly determine risks, do what they can to minimize them, and then move forward with a bold plan despite the remaining risks. Entrepreneurs function with a higher sense of "I can change the outcome" than most other LEMONs, the exception being the Organizer.

We interviewed a self-described Entrepreneur once who explained all the startups with which he had been involved. When it came time to discuss compensation, he didn't have a risky bone in his body. He wanted his entire salary fixed with no possible upside for performance. He was not an Entrepreneur.

Entrepreneurs have the ability to move at a rapid pace from one opportunity to the next. When you meet Entrepreneurs that are "between opportunities" don't expect them to be considering only one option at a time. And if something doesn't pan out, they possess the ability to move or to morph the opportunity to something that is viable. (Luminaries are not wild about others who morph their ideas; Entrepreneurs see it as essential to progress.)

Taking out trash, kissing feet

Entrepreneurs may not be able to swing a machete or use a nail gun, but they are the practical people when it comes to clearing the obstacles and building the basics of a business. Having done the mental preparation in filtering an opportunity and deciding whether it is worth pursuing, they can pull things together. They focus on the crucial early action items that are needed, and put their own shoulder to the wheel. Entrepreneurs put the basic building blocks in place that are necessary to seize an opportunity.

During the early stages of a company, Entrepreneurs do anything: they figure out the office (or garage) space, interview staff, design logos, articulate vision, set up the financial records, define corporate values, take out the trash … you name it. They do this not because they relish the work but because they are willing to do whatever it takes. An Entrepreneur-Luminary friend who formulates ideas and then forms engineering teams to make them happen says, "My job is to kiss the feet of the engineers."

First heat, then light

Passion. Once Entrepreneurs have set their minds on something, they believe in it, and they build up visible passion. This creates a level of energy that others warm to; E-followers soon find themselves infected with the same passion. There is no question in anyone's mind that a successful Entrepreneur is 110% committed. They want to be the best at something, and it shows. After General Motors acquired EDS, Ross Perot found himself on the GM board and is purported to have asked a question that nonplussed the GM-ers.. "Can't we be the best at something? If we can't have the best car, can't we have the best cigarette lighter or door handle?" Entrepreneurs have to have something they can be excited about.

Good Entrepreneurs create emotional attachments with their support teams and it is not uncommon for key people to follow serial-entrepreneurs from one opportunity to the next. After a while the team can have an attachment to the Entrepreneur herself and whatever she does next.

Entrepreneurs do not have failures, they just have "learning experiences." Entrepreneurs bounce back. They are resilient, refusing to wallow in setbacks, not allowing their hearts to get discouraged. How do you view failure? What impact have past failures had on how you see your future?

Managers: Stable Able, Steady Eddie

Sticktoitiveness. Managers have it in spades. Where Luminaries and Entrepreneurs love doing things the first time, Managers love working out the kinks and getting people who can get it done again and again and again. Managers, when honest, are more comfortable the third time round.

Managers know how many minutes there are in an hour. They have somehow grasped the fact that the clock does not magically stop just because I received a phone call on the way out or drove past a sale I couldn't resist. Cautious Managers are the ones who drive the route to an important appointment the day before so that they know where they are going and how long it takes, adjusting for time of day and weather conditions.

Managers have also come to grips with the laws of Cause and Effect. (Luminaries invent another law to supersede this one. Entrepreneurs say, "Well, they told me X was impossible and I did it anyway." And Networkers simply suspend reality for a while… sometimes a long while.) But Managers know reality from unreality.

Managers plan, and good managers plan well, and well in advance. They can stay the course on planning that takes time, reworking something until an acceptable level of completion has been achieved. They have the patience to flesh-out ideas and work through what their implications might be on all aspects of the organization.

Managers usually have the best understanding of organizational processes and procedures. They can define a process that will ensure a predictable result. Then they can build a skilled team to execute the process repeatedly.

I'll get back to you

Given the aversion that Managers have to "just winging it" they tend to develop a specialty or strength in at least one area. It may not be the area that they end up managing, but they like to have one under the belt – "I have done it." They tend to blow less smoke about their capabilities.

Their high degree of realism causes them to have a good understanding of the assets needed to build in a way that gets good results. Before committing to having something done, a Manager will assess the resource requirements. They count the bricks before they start building the wall.

Managers do things with more consistency than others. When they say they will do something, you can count on them. If you ask them to do something, rather than say "Yes" because that is the answer you want, a solid Manager will go home, count the cost, consider the resource requirements, build in a 10% contingency, and then give you a considered answer.

Under authority, with authority

One of the wonderful strengths about Managers is their recognition of and acceptance of authority. They understand what it means to be under authority, they are happy to be directed, and consequently they are able to exercise authority clearly and without clutter. A clear example of this is recorded in ancient literature when a Roman military officer approached Jesus Christ about healing a sick servant. Here's the dialogue as recorded by Eugene Peterson.

> "Master, my servant is sick. He can't walk. He's in terrible pain."
> Jesus said, "I'll come and heal him."
> "Oh, no," said the captain, "I don't want to put you to all that trouble; just give the order and my servant will be fine. I'm a man who takes orders and gives orders. I tell one soldier, 'Go,' and he goes; to another, 'Come,' and he comes; to my slave, 'Do this,' and he does it.'"

This strength of Managers gives them an ability to respect the authority of others and to exercise authority with respect.

Managers answer questions based on what they think is right, and not based on what they think you want to hear. (That would be the Networker.) They tend to take things literally. When you ask a Manager a question, they are more focused on the content of what you ask and not the body language, tone of voice, or motives behind the kingdom.

Order is generally important to Managers. They feel better when there is some logic, some flow, some rationale for the way things happen. The discipline of Managers allows them to do the things that are necessary to keep their world in order.

Managers are often good coaches who can come alongside people where they are and patiently move them along. They slowly build long-term working relationships that stand the test of time.

Managers are not easily offended. This is a great asset to them and the community, family or organization of which they are a part. When one of the other LEONs has flared up and gone back the next day to apologize, the Manager either does not remember the incident or has no problem extending forgiveness.

Reality Index

Finally—and this could be a Head, Hand or Heart strength—Managers have what I call The Reality Index set to True North, to center. They have the most grounded sense of what is real. The Luminary and Networkers are too optimistic. The Organizers are too pessimistic. The Entrepreneur could go either way. But the Manager is the sane one at the party.

Reality Index

If you are not a Manager, try to find out how many degrees off center you are calibrated, and then make adjustments or run your plans and ideas past a Manager to get them trued up with reality.

Organizer: The Vision-Implication connection

It seems too simple to say that Organizers see the practical implications of other people's vision. Crucial to the long-term success of a venture is someone who can answer the question, "What does this mean today?" While Luminaries (in particular) and even Entrepreneurs and Managers can be comfortable in their paper plans for a season, Organizers know that if A, B and C don't get done this week, all those plans will be worthless.

Organizers think clearly about what it takes to make things happen. They put verbs in the sentences of the other leaders. Their systems may seem rudimentary to the more schooled leader, but they work for the Organizer.

Organizers can cut through a maze of woolly thinking and get to the "What" quickly. When not overloaded, they can extract the core tasks to be done today. Unfortunately, Organizers may not always articulate their intuition about issues rapidly or clearly, so others may gloss over them, but they know when something isn't going to fly, when "that dawg won't hunt."

Just did it

Organizers work. They are not afraid to tackle a job, to start something, to take practical action. In the 1930's my grandfather was a preacher in London and he received a "call" from a church in South Africa which required moving his wife and five children a long way in a small boat for a long time. While he was praying about what decision to make, my grandmother was packing. Organizers take action.

Organizers don't spend too much time gloating over the task they just completed. They will step back, be satisfied, and move on. They quickly get to the critical tasks needed for their version of the 70% solution.

Organizers are often good at and content with temporary fixes. While this would drive someone else crazy, it works for the Organizer. Back to Mabel, my grandmother. At some stage she had all of her teeth removed in one sitting—those were the days—and my grandfather had some ministerial convention he had planned. Problem was that Mabel's teeth hadn't arrived yet. So she refused to do the organizing for the convention until she had teeth. My grandfather (the Luminary waiting for the perfect set of teeth) acquiesced, the dentist quickly made a set of temporary choppers—not even a 70% solution—and Mabel died with them still in her mouth about fifty years later. The temporary fix worked, and she was happy.

Organizers can spot and usually resolve practical "issues" quickly. I say "issues" because it is possible that not everything an Organizer sees as an issue is in fact an issue. (No surprises here: not every "brilliant" idea that the Luminary has is brilliant; not every "great opportunity" an Entrepreneur chases is great, or an opportunity; not every process instituted by a Manager is necessary; not every new contact of a Networker is a good contact.) We will dig into this more when we get to the Weaknesses of LEMONs.

Built to serve

At the heart level, Organizers are quick to embrace the dreams and opportunities and plans of others. Once their basic, practical questions have been put to rest, they trust that the others have done their job thinking it through, and they take ownership quickly.

In the early days of a venture they are easily motivated. They don't have to be mollycoddled into getting up every morning and putting in a good days work. They don't need the constant reminders about what to do.

Organizers have an intuitive sense of the needs and wants of others. They ask questions, watch facial expressions, and listen for the unspoken wants of people in a group. They take mental note of what they can quietly do themselves to address these preferences, and they productively bring those things to the surface that are the responsibility of others in the group. Organizers don't need to be in the limelight, but their sense of right causes them to raise their voice on behalf of others who may be overlooked.

They like to see people getting along (as do Networkers) and are alert to interpersonal matters that could get in the way of forward progress. (Healthy Organizers are not overly sensitive and don't stop the bus every time someone could potentially feel carsick.)

The bottom line nice thing about Organizers is this: they have servant's hearts. They genuinely love to serve others. They are happy to help, happy to do things for others, and content with exercising their gifts of practical service. This need not make them doormats or dumping grounds for bad jobs that no one else wants. They can have personal parameters and exercise choice. In the end, however, Organizers choose to serve. And this, in part, is what makes them indispensable leaders, because a leadership group without roots in service is not far from tyranny.

Easily connect with...	Ideas	Resources	Processes	Issues	People

Networkers: Connecting the dots

Networkers understand what makes people tick. When they come into a group they are quick to fathom the interpersonal dynamics, where the people are in regards to the agenda, and who is in charge. They know who makes the real decisions, and they work their way into the confidences of such people. They find out what people need—whether friendship, knowledge, information, alliances, a cup of coffee—and become the source of provision.

In the broader scope of things, Networkers see the tremendous possibilities that come from linking people and organizations together in networks or ecosystems. The skilled Networker can deliberately design and build conglomerates of interconnected entities that come together to fulfill a purpose. John Chambers of Cisco Systems is one such example of an acquisition prone CEO who deliberately builds corporate networks. One of the frustrations of Networkers—and this is not a weakness on their parts—is that most organizations do not do well at partnering. This does not stop the avid Networker from trying. To the rest of the LEMOs, the value of weaving a spider web between disparate people and entities is questionable. To a Networker, it is concrete.

Priming the network

Like pumps, networks need to be primed. Individuals and organizations gravitate towards being internally focused, and this causes the decay of external relationships. Networkers know this and have an intuitive sense of when to call people to keep the network primed. Just about the time you are thinking, "I haven't heard from him for a long time," the phone rings.

When Networkers have a free moment, they contact people. This is a strength. They are tireless in weaving webs. Like their creature cousins, the spiders, if they wake up and find the web knocked down, they just make another one. And like the spider, they are not sure what may land in the web, but they know that if they have it stretched out there something is bound to come along and get caught.

My new best friend

A common comment about Networkers is that they make everyone feel like his or her best friend... in five minutes. "I feel like I have known her forever." (Warning: you haven't.) But it still feels like it, and the Networker means it when they declare newfound love, and we all feel the love. Such is the heart strength of Networkers.

Networkers are often natural encouragers. They love to spur others on, get touched by stories of how struggling people succeeded, and are natural promoters of the abilities and talents of others. Don't just think of them as salespeople who say nice things to close a deal. Networkers sell even when there is no money involved because they are the mouthpieces for the parts of society that won't or cannot speak for themselves. When a Networker comes back from an overseas vacation, the pictures are of people, but not just any people: the poor, the old, the unusual, the overlooked… these are all folks that find a space in the photo album of the Networker.

The writer says, "Love covers a multitude of sins." Networkers know this, and a strength that follows is that they can sustain relationships because people cut them a lot of slack since they are loveable and loving. They connect well at a heart level, and this gets them a lot of grace.

Adding up your Strengths

Look back on the chapter and count the strengths that you exhibit for each LEMON type. Record them in the table below.

L	E	M	O	N

Total score on strengths – transfer to Your LEMON Profile in the Appendix.

Chapter 09
Bitter Lemon

The
weaknesses
of LEMONs

*W*eaknesses are often the flipsides of our strengths. With the giftedness that each of us has received comes a set of areas that can be detrimental to ourselves and especially to those whom we lead.

Even on a good day we will have these tendencies, so we must understand them if we are to mitigate them. These weaknesses of LEMONs are not sinister; they are tendencies to be noted and worked against even when we are doing a good job as leaders. (On a bad-leadership-day these will be exacerbated by a phenomenon that I call "The Dark Side of LEMON Leadership." This is covered in a later chapter.)

Some LEMONs are more apt to recognize their leadership DNA through the strengths, but many get a good read on themselves by identifying with the weaknesses of LEMONs. Once again, these are stated in somewhat absolute terms in order to be clear and helpful. There are exceptions to any of the weaknesses; don't take offence, take in the general patterns, combine them with the strengths, and learn what this says about you and the people you know.

LEMON TRUISM: The defining strength that gives impetus to a person, organization or movement in the early days can become the Achilles heel.

Luminaries: Cross-eyed focus

For all the thinking done by Luminaries, it is easy for them to become narrowly focused on their own ideas. They can lose the thread of what others are thinking if they become reclusive, particularly if they do not deliberately relate to a broader audience. Luminaries with a "head weakness" usually become proprietary in their thinking, losing the natural curiosity and the desire to learn from others. When outside context is lost, then the danger of faulty thinking escalates. If they have resources, they end up burning good money on bad ideas. Focus becomes myopia when Luminaries loose touch with other LEMONs or the outside world.

The flipside of their strength of being able to stay the course over decades is that they can hold onto dead ideas too long. (Entrepreneurs and Networkers would have moved on long ago; Organizers would not have cared about the ideas anyway.) There are few things sadder than once-were-Luminaries on small islands riding near dead horses, in circles.

The alternate (to riding dead idea horses) is that they jump from one idea horse to another too quickly without setting a strategic context whereby others in the organization can evaluate the latest direction of the herd. They are, as someone has put it, Idea Hamsters. The president of a company exhausted his organization by sharing random product ideas with passing staff (in the spirit of dialogue, in his mind) only to find that his comments were taken as mandates to launch new product development initiatives. No wonder they were selling competing products to the same customers from different silos in the company. The Luminary felt compelled to stay abreast of the market (which was, by definition, out in the future, given his depth of field) while the company was begging him to stop spewing out new ideas. Luminaries can exhaust their teams with new things. If you are a Luminary use discretion and don't say everything you know.

Another weakness of Luminaries is Warp Speed. It may be a strength when you are working at a laboratory bench or buried in research, but when you are a leader of an organization it is generally a weakness. Leaders serve, and you cannot serve others if they cannot keep up. You are only leading when you have some people following you. A confused group squinting at the horizon where they thought they last saw your dust, is not a following.

Finally, Luminaries who try to do it all themselves (either for fear that someone is out to steal their ideas, or for frustration that their colleagues don't move fast enough) end up being isolated from the members of the team whom they desperately need. "I just want Accounting to take care of the nest so that I can fly like an eagle with my next great idea."

Disconnects, handoffs, and Luminary intensity

Many Luminaries become disconnected from the organization they lead. One reason for this is that they hand-off responsibility for things they have incubated before their thinking has developed enough or permeated the organization. Put another way, they fail to make the connection between the way they view life and the way their organization should run at a nuts and bolts level. I got to know one of the leading thinkers in America on culture and worldview. The organization he founded is influenced by his values, but the Operating Model is virtually untouched by this profound thinking. (Were he a Luminary-Manager or perhaps a Luminary-Organizer this would not be the case. I suspect he is a Luminary-Networker, and this in itself can lead to nefarious outcomes.)

You don't have to look far for examples of prominent Luminaries who have received a new call or seen a new rabbit. Their focus shifts almost immediately to that new thing. They dream about it, speak about it, and convince others of its global importance. Then they up and leave. They think they spent plenty of time in transition. In reality they made some speeches, quickly found a successor, but spent little time thinking about a thorough handoff. They often leave a trail of dropped batons and broken Balance Sheets behind them.

Some Luminaries, like Entrepreneurs, are intense. Furthermore, some are intensely fast, and others are intensely deep. A weakness of Luminaries is assuming that everyone else has the same intensity as they do, and they therefore don't adjust the "clock speed" or "depth charge" to that of their colleagues. A man I know once said to a Luminary-deep friend, "You are so deep!" With a knowing look she replied, "Sometimes I wish I was shallow like you."

Luminaries can also delay dealing with practical issues which they know are there because they believe that "if we all get enough of the right principles, these issues will take care of themselves."

So things that could have been noted, added to an Issues Log, and raised at the next meeting are deferred in the hopes that they resolve themselves. Occasionally they do, but mostly they don't.

Rejected ideas, ejected people

Luminaries easily write off those who do not track with their ideas. They put them in the "Don't bother to go there" pile. While Luminaries usually have a long relational fuse, they can get a mental block about someone for any number of reasons, and that is it. End of story. The big underlying reason is often a clash of philosophies, not personalities. The public and acrimonious feuds between Luminaries are fueled partly by an endless supply of ego, and partly by philosophy. Witness the "no love lost" scenario of the software titans.

Another factor can be that Luminaries don't do too well with those who are slow on the uptake. Just as Entrepreneurs are like bees going from flower to flower looking for the best opportunities, so an unsettled Luminary will float between people or groups until he finds those that are in sync with his ideas. In a think tank environment Luminaries are flattered by people debating their ideas; in a production environment they are not enthralled with those who question the merit of the ideas.

Where a Luminary is leading the organization, they usually don't want to give others time to process their ideas. When the Luminary is finished thinking then, in their book, the thinking is done. Now it should be on to implementation and it should not be the time for a re-hashing of the ideas. This can be particularly problematic if the Luminary is a solo processor because others are not brought into the dialogue soon enough.

Luminaries can fail to see that the lack of enthusiasm is not necessarily a matter of people being in disagreement with their dreams or ideas. They can mistakenly assume that lack of immediate acceptance is non-acceptance, and they do not stay the distance in allowing others to come on board.

This is one of the reasons that Luminaries often don't make money out of their own ideas. They are too impatient to wait the five years (or whatever their particular Luminary Horizon may be) until the general public is willing to accept something and it can be commercialized. Not only does this trait lose money, it also loses friends.

A final heart weakness that I will touch on here is that Luminaries who happen also to be in the Genius IQ range are not always socially smart, to put it nicely. They have the right analysis but lack diplomacy. They have IQ, but not EQ. The same news delivered by a Networker and a Luminary could sound like the difference between an invitation to a Caribbean Cruise and a long walk to the woodshed.

Entrepreneurs and The Big Picture

Entrepreneurs are really good at some things, and a key to their success is selling those few things to investors, customers and employees as if they are everything. They have to be focused, and it doesn't help to sell the areas of weakness, so they sell their strengths. The downside is that they can come to believe their own advertising and become blinded by their strengths in one or two areas. The strengths are so strong that they can no longer see their weaknesses.

A variant on this is that Entrepreneurs don't necessarily see the "big picture" when compared to the perspective that Luminaries and Managers have. We will explore this more when we look at the matter of Vision and how this looks different for each of the LEMONs. The flipside of their strength of focus is that, in order to be successful, Entrepreneurs deal with a slice of reality and glance over the rest as if it is of no consequence.

A head weakness of Entrepreneurs is that their optimism causes them to see opportunities where there are none. That which they can see as a sure deal is, in fact, no deal at all.
Entrepreneurs seldom fail; they just have learning experiences.

This philosophy carries the danger that they ignore setbacks altogether, move into denial, and lose the assets of adversity past.

I can do it... intuitively

It is well known that Entrepreneurs not only don't have some of the polished skills of experts in particular fields, but they may also not need them in the early stages. If an Entrepreneur disdains others who do have these skills, however, then they will not learn from them, and will further lack the depth of competence to see where professional management is needed. This is double trouble because it stunts the natural curiosity of a good learner, and it hampers their career path. This is recognized by venture capitalists (VCs) who often replace Entrepreneurs with professional managers as the corporation grows. I am not necessarily in favor of this practice, but it is understandable, particularly when the E fails to invest in the growth of personal skills beyond their narrow slice.

LEMON TRUISM: Prizing intuition above the disciplines of maturity can be fatal... and vice versa.

Networkers and Organizers don't like the stricture of processes, procedures, and policies. They don't read the corporate operating manuals as a pastime. Given their finely developed intuition about tasks and "To Do's," they prefer to work on autopilot. The downside is that their failures can be predictable because they refuse to engage in the behaviors that will overcome innate weaknesses.

Entrepreneurs can fake skills when they have to, and if this becomes a habit, it can mean that they fail to grow skills. The good Entrepreneurs know their craft and are students about their work and deliberate in skills development. These aren't the skills of a

Manager or Networker; they are the craft of the Entrepreneur.

Entrepreneurs can delay facing issues because "When we get enough money and momentum, this will go away." You might argue that this is in fact exercising the skill of "planned neglect" where the less important is allowed to fall by the wayside. The temptation for an Entrepreneur is to suspect reality and hope that the problem takes care of itself. They would be good to heed the warning, "Depend on the rabbit's foot if you will, but remember that it did not work for the rabbit."

Get on board or get out of the way

The ability of Entrepreneurs to generate excitement about their latest passion has, of course, a downside. Those who don't want to play on their team or jump on their latest opportunity are quickly passed over. I remember being approached by someone who wanted to stage the corporate equivalent of a palace coup. "Are you on board?" he asked, after all of five minutes of explanation. When I wanted to think about his rapidly hatched plan overnight, this was taken as a "No."

Every one of the LEMONs can commit the crime of seeing people as resources to be used, and each of us does it for a differing set of reasons. The Entrepreneur falls into this trap precisely because they are good at gathering resources and bringing people on board. When they forget that companies are there to build people as much as people are there to build companies, then they fall into the people trap.

LEMON TRUISM: Using people to build organizations isn't half as fulfilling as using organizations to build people.

Creative Managers: there's an idea

Some Managers lack the creativity and spontaneity of other LEONs. Other people can see this better than the Managers do, just like the time I pulled up in front of a large insurance company that was not an audit client of mine. In fact, I was there to discuss some consulting work. As I got out of the car the security guard strolled over to me and said, "The auditor parking is at the back of the building." I was such an auditor I could not see it, but to the guard it was as clear as the stripes on my three-piece suit.

If you are a Manager you may be screaming at the page, "I do have ideas. I am creative!" You are correct: everyone has an element of creativity. It is just that we are creative about different things. A good friend works at Pixar helping create movies like Finding Nemo and Monsters, Inc. The folks at Pixar are creative, and although my friend may only work on the left eyelid of the fourth fish in the seaweed scene, kids think he is a rock star. People who are creative about process improvements on supply chain systems don't get the same adulation. Is one more creative than another? Not necessarily. But one is perceived as being more creative. The danger for the Manager is that, rather than celebrate the areas in which they are creative—the development of processes, people, organizations—they scorn ideas not their own. They would rather stick to things that they have already adopted (thereby reinforcing their discipline and consistency) than take on some brilliant idea that a less-than-realistic person formulated.

Managers do not like 'failure' because it makes them seem like they haven't done their planning. They pride themselves on planning, so when something goes wrong they can be tempted to suppress the bad news if it makes it seem that they didn't do their planning.

Managers can delay facing issues because "we have a process, and the process should take care of it on its own." But processes without people often fail, and Managers are expert at knowing how to circumvent, ignore or avoid the processes that they set up in the first place. This is one of the reasons we have Space Shuttle disasters: we have rooms full of Managers, binders full of processes, warning systems up the wall and down, and yet the flipside of our strength, left unchecked, ruins us. Ironically, Managers think the system will prevent all problems, and hate to admit that the design of the system was incomplete.

Processes are there to liberate

Many Managers fail to grasp that processes, policies and procedures are there to free people up to be all that they should be. When Managers think that their job is to enforce the procedures, then they become rigid and force others to play by the rules (which the Manager wrote, of course). They can catch people on technicalities ("The Expense Policy says…") better than anyone. Managers can use Policies, Processes, etc. as a big stick rather than as a safety net. They can become more engrossed in the letter of the law than the spirit of the law. Sometimes this is essential, but often it is a matter of "control on steroids."

> **LEMON TRUISM: The real job of someone skilled in processes is to continually refresh them so that the processes make life easier for highly motivated people to do and be their best.**

When the bottom line is a barrier

Managers care about people, they develop people, and they can have lifelong best friends. But their directness and no-nonsense approach can cause others to perceive them as being cool and calculating. When the way in which they describe an emotional topic is in terms of cost-benefit and bottom line impacts, this really presses the buttons of non-Managers. For example, when the Networker asks, "What do you feel about the poor folks in Marketing who got laid off?" and the Manager replies, "I think it will add about 2.75% to the bottom line." Not good.

Someone has observed that people have two walls built around their hearts, each wall being a different height. In some cultures the external wall is low; you make friends immediately, share your deep secrets with someone in the line at the movie theater, and yet you have a high internal wall. The unsuspecting low-wall hurdler then runs smack into the 50-foot high inner wall—welcome to California—and has a hard time getting to know you. In other countries the external wall is high which means it takes a long time to get to know someone, but once you are over that wall the interior wall is low, a lifelong relationship is formed, and you can look forward to lots of good German beer. This analogy is true of the different LEMONs. Networkers have a marginal exterior wall, and Managers have a high exterior wall. The high level of integrity of a Manager—refusing to say they are committed unless they really are—can create barriers to intimacy. What could be a healthy caution becomes an obstacle to relationship.

A Manager faces a real danger when it comes to weighing the motives of those not complying with "the rules." He or she assumes that others actually see things their way, but are ignoring common sense. Managers assume that everyone else knows exactly what is supposed to be done and how to do things "the right way" but they—the LEONs—are just being rebellious. Through dialogue I have found that LEON and friends never even thought about the M's processes, let alone spent the whole night scheming about how to break the rules just to annoy Mr. M.

Managers can set high expectations that no one can meet. We are not talking about interpersonal relationship expectations where people are hoping for the perfect boss, wife or spiritual leader. We are talking about performance expectations where the Big M is looking for 100% performance.

Who wants to be a Managaire?

Leaving the world of 100% we come to Organizer Land where 70% is good enough. Sometimes this works, but in the land of parachutes, aircraft mechanics and brain surgery, 70% could be disastrous.

For all their ability to focus, Organizers need to guard against the danger of dropping the ball on multiple areas when they are zoned in on the task at hand. The downside of the ability to focus is a lack of consideration for the schedule of others, and a neglect of the other responsibilities that they carry. So if an Organizer has decided that the most important task to them is wrapping gifts for a party, they can completely zone out any other jobs and people aside from that singularly "important" task. This tendency includes suspending the reality that there are tasks from business-as-usual that have to be taken care of. When challenged they retort, "I can't be perfect."

Organizers have explained to me that they can multi-task, but to a point. Each Organizer (and anyone who works closely with them) needs to know whether they can handle three or nine or twenty-three things at once... then stay away from the limit. If the limit is nine, make sure you have no more than 7 things going. (Hint: for the LENs tempted to push the limits just because boundaries are there to be broken and mountains are there to be climbed... don't go there: it is in no one's best interest to have an Organizer beyond their multi-tasking range.)

Organizers are great at spotting issues but when they cross the line to the dark side they can just as easily create issues where there are none. Sometimes this is to be indispensable or in control, but often it is just done out of habit. They can take molehills and turn them into mountains quicker than anyone can come up with a plan to move the mountains.

Because Organizers are happy to serve and get a kick out of spotting a problem and fixing it, they can fail to put boundaries around their job. This can cause them to get burned out, and this is bad enough. What is worse is that they can meander into everyone else's work. Few things are off limits to an Organizer who roves around finding blockages in the corporate plumbing and shoving hand grenades up the pipes to fix things.

Some Organizers cannot envision a peaceful world. When things get too quiet for too long they take this as a sign that things need a little stirring up. This might not be all bad, but for the Organizer as a person it can lead to a tendency to self-destruct. They can develop a pattern of sabotaging their own success. So when their career starts going too smoothly they raise a little hell and start a few battles. That way they don't have to grow into new responsibilities and become, heaven forbid, a Manager.

Don't give me training, give me space

There is a strong connection between Organizers who downplay the capabilities of others and those who are unwilling to round out their own capabilities. Organizers can perpetuate personal deficits because they don't want to put out the effort that it will take to move from the unconscious competence to a conscious competence. They can get around their need for development by neutering the systems of others. Their defense is, "I can do this intuitively." If you are an Organizer and you actually read the instruction manuals that come with the things you purchase, you probably don't have to worry about this weakness.

Organizers can put spanners in spokes rather than build wheels. Knowing that they have the practical know-how to make things happen (and others may not), they use this to hang onto skills rather than build such skills in others.

Velcro and prickly people

You will recall that Organizers don't care too much for title or status. You are doomed, however, if you mistake this for them not needing appreciation. All of us like to be appreciated, and this is no less true for Organizers. The error we make is that we think that because they don't want a title they don't have needs. If they are not given the few essentials that they need to function effectively (in their book), then they can turn sour, and the organization pays the price.

Have you ever noticed a person who needs "just one thing" to make them happy? (I am not talking about one of the Seven Great Lies of the world: "I only need this one thing to complete my wardrobe.") It may be a child who has determined that they need their own room, or a colleague who needs a dedicated phone line. Organizers can fixate on this one thing until the absence of it makes their life miserable. And yours.

When a loyal Organizer becomes detached from the primary leader whom they are serving, they shift from protecting that leader and begin to protect themselves. They systematically do things that ensure that, over time, they build loyalty to themselves rather than their organization. Instead of covering the back of the rest of the leadership team, they expose it to the corporate elements.

A related tendency of Organizers is that they get in the middle of emotional topics. They mistake their strength in understanding people's feelings as being a license to become the emotional filter between different layers of the organization. (Note the duality: they don't want anyone between themselves and the leader, but they are happy to be the go-between.) They entrench their position as trusted aid by having people come to them rather than "bother the leader." Or instead of just recognizing discord and resolving it, they plant seeds of discord and fuel it.

In any organization people instinctively know who to go to when they have a complaint. It is not the Human Resources department or the Complaints Department; it is the nearest Organizer. Organizers with heart conditions become office Velcro – dirt just sticks to them.

If Managers believe that they have the best grasp of reality, Organizers believe that they are the ones that really "make things work." It stands to reason that they can feel under-appreciated for their unseen role. ("If I left...") The truth is, none of us is indispensable, not even the Organizer. But, for the rest of us, the sad fact is that Organizers often are under-appreciated because, until now, we have not had a separate definition of their vital role.

The strength of an Organizer in serving anonymously also means that they can do things to sabotage an organization, and do so somewhat undetected. They can operate under the radar, and this can cut both ways.

As we know, Organizers love to bring things to closure. There are some things, however, that are best left to unfold and develop. Organizers need to develop the ability to let time do the work on some people and situations, resisting the urge to have a confrontational meeting every time they notice an issue. Organizers keep short accounts, and this is good. But part of developing people is letting them run with a loose rein for a season.

Rosy Reality

Networkers can be way out in right field—the Luminaries already have left field covered —when it comes to assessing reality. The glass-twice-full tendencies of Networkers together with their exuberant belief in good things happening, tends to dull the edge of critical thinking.

The strength of Networkers is that they quickly connect with the ideas of others, see the good points, and link them to other good ideas. The downside of this is that they tend to suffer from Vision de Jour. The vision that they hold can easily be the vision of the last person who was in their office. If you have had five sets of strategy consultants in as many years, beware. If you have changed direction to mimic your CEO golfing friends, beware. If you are animated after a conversation with a guru, give yourself a five day cooling off period before you commit resources to going in his direction.

It is true that a key role of leaders is to set the context in which their organizations operate. The problem for Networkers is that they can struggle to do this because they vacillate on vision unless that vision is directly consistent with their Networker strengths. Such a vision they can stick to, but when they are espousing the vision of the day, then they fail to set context.

The Leader's Radar

While on the topic of the blind spots of Networkers I have to pause for a moment to shed light on the Radar of LEMONs. I met an air traffic controller some years ago who explained his job in some detail. He worked on the busiest air corridor in the world, the route between the San Francisco Bay Area and the Los Angeles Area. Planes come and go constantly. He gave hair-raising accounts about how they occasionally "lost" planes and regaled us with near miss stories. LEMONs also have internal radar that is used more for communications than for vision. In front of them is a screen and they have different methods of spotting who is coming onto their radar and how they can best communicate with or avoid them. Some use trusted executive assistants. Others use electronic scanning devices such as email, voicemail and personal digital assistants. It was through observation of Networkers that I first got attuned to this notion of radar.

There are three key elements of the LEMON leader's radar:

1. How much of the radar the leader can have in view at one time.

2. If they cannot keep the whole radar in view, the breadth and speed of rotation of the scanning slice of the radar, and

3. What happens to the rest of the radar… the part that is in the dark.

As the radar scans, the leader picks up those needing outgoing communications and those sending incoming communications. The leader chooses to respond to what he or she sees based on a number of criteria, some of them personal, and some corporate.

Type of leader	What they see	What happens to the rest
Luminary	They can see the whole radar from a distance, but are not always tuned into the details. They filter out people that don't tie into the Luminary agenda.	They can miss some of the dimmer signals, ignore the details, and overlook things that are important but not urgent. They can also screen out details that might bog them down.
Entrepreneur	They are tuned into the critical few things that are needed right now. While they cannot see the whole picture at once, their slice spins so quickly they effectively take a pass at all crucial areas frequently.	The rest is in the dark: call it planned neglect.
Manager	They see much of the radar, if not all of it, and see it closer than the Luminary. Their scanner moves more slowly than the Entrepreneur.	They have systems to track things that fall off the radar. They have scouts or monitors who bring things to them in an exception basis. They get to people based on duty, good practices and integrity to themselves and others.

Type of leader	What they see	What happens to the rest
Organizers	They have a relatively narrow scanner that spins quickly. They look for issues. Their strength in keeping things working causes them to be more deliberate in checking in on points on the radar whether there is a current problem or not.	When you are in the dark with an Organizer it is usually because they are preoccupied with a task. Don't take it personally.
Networkers	They see just one slice at a time. It rotates at varying speeds, but not quick enough to guarantee that all bases will be covered. They see those people who are in their slice intently. They interact with them frequently, have warm communications, seem like best friends…	…until they drop off the radar. When a Networker wants you on the radar, there you are. When they don't, you are in the dark. And the fact is, you don't know when the scanner will come back your way. When you are in the dark with a Networker it is because they are preoccupied with someone else. In the sales world you might say they know how to qualify opportunities and move on to the promising ones. Another way to say it is that they easily drop people who are not advancing their agenda, or if someone more interesting comes along.

I have met many heartbroken people whose best friend has moved on. They were close colleagues, tighter than tighter, friendlier than friends. But they have not heard from their Networker friend in months, maybe years. When I have explained the "off radar" wiring of Networkers the jilted people at least get some comfort.

Black Holes and Bad News

So a weakness for Networkers is that they have communication black holes. People and topics can easily go 'off radar' with Networkers. I have seen this to be true for some of the other LEMONs, but with Networkers it is epidemic.

Networkers need to be liked. The effect of this is that they don't like to deliver bad news. If this becomes a habit, then over time, they no longer see bad news coming. When everything is going well the Networker is predisposed to keep the good news flowing. When the Networker's view of reality is challenged by, say, a Manager or an Organizer, it is easier for the Networker to shoot the messenger than hear bad news.

The paradox is that Networkers are naturally the most open to input, feedback, or criticism. But if the strength of the Networker's wiring overrides their ability to take action based on the input they receive, then their openness to input means little. There is a world of difference between being open to input and seeing the implications of such input.

Networkers like everyone to be happy, they like to keep the peace, and they are prone to avoiding confrontation. They are not great at administering discipline or corrective action. Networkers delay facing issues today because they think, "with enough grace, these issues will go away." Sometimes this is true, but a Networker has to discern when it is a gracious delay, and when it is avoiding the issue.

Finally, while a strength of Networkers is that they warm to others' ideas, the corollary is that they borrow thinking from others without realizing it. Networkers go from

"As Sir Winston Churchill said in his book…" to
> "I once read…" to
>> "As I have always said…" in about a week.

Getting it done

The good thing about Networkers is that they usually know that they need help to get things done, and they are not afraid to call on others for assistance. Left to their own devices, however, Networkers can have poor follow through on practical tasks. Their actions can appear to be random if they are not part of a team that complements their capabilities.

Because the Networker has a more loose definition of work when it comes to the core tasks of an organization (and a tighter definition on the relational matters) it is possible, if not likely, that they think that things are getting done when they are not. They have problems being practical, not in the home improvement context, but in the running of organizations. A Networker therefore needs to double-check with other LEMONs to ensure that their definition of "It's complete!" is acceptable.

Networkers are often successful at winning the trust of clients and other leaders. But if they take on too much responsibility in attempting to become the confidant and loyal meeter-of-needs, they get over-committed. They are therefore not able to deliver what they promise, and this damages their credibility. Or they deliver what's expected, but burn themselves out doing so.

Networkers seldom know when too many people is enough. They can overload meetings with conflicting agendas. They invite one person to a meeting with one idea of a meeting's agenda, then meet someone in the street who "obviously" is connected, so they get invited too and the original intent of the meeting is lost. This wastes the time of others and burns the Networker's relational capital.

I'll get back to you

Networkers are often the source of great social connections. They arrange parties, pull groups together, and act as the social glue between friends.

There are also times when Networkers do what is socially expedient rather than what is right. If you invite them to a party, they give you a sense that they may be there, but do not actually so "Yes." Or you might hear "No" at the last minute and be confused as to why they took so long in making a decision. Some observations about the social arrangements of Networkers will give insight into their DNA:

- They can fit more things into their calendar than the rest of the leaders can, and do so without feelings stressed.
- They delay sharing bad news. If "No, I am not coming to your party" sounds like bad news, they hold off on communicating this. In their minds, a miracle may happen and things will open up, so why close the door when maybe they could attend all three parties?
- They leave people hanging, awaiting responses while they scan the social horizon to assess all their options.
- Speaking of options, Networkers like to leave arrangements loose until the last minute so that they can keep their alternatives open in case something better comes along. Have you have ever wondered why Joe Networker didn't get back to you to confirm whether he would be there for your gala opening? It is simple: he is keeping his options open in case a better invitation comes along. By telling you nothing, he retains his flexibility. You could easily get them there by telling them that other important people will be there, of course.
- Networkers read people like books, so can have a tendency to say what they think you want to hear. It is more important to be liked than to tell it like it is. Rather than say, "There is no way I could attend your function," they say they will attend, but don't.

- They assume that everyone has the same tolerance for ambiguity. Networkers can be more specific about what it takes to have a successful social event that other leaders; they are specific about this. But they have a greater tolerance for ambiguity than others when it comes to life in general. You don't really need to know too many details... hang loose, would you?

Networkers-gone-bitter believe that once they have made a relationship, they "own" it. That relationship becomes part of their network; it is their relationship, their friendship and woe to those who "use" their network. Remember, Networkers protect their network as fiercely as Luminaries protect ideas, Entrepreneurs protect opportunities, Managers protect processes, and Organizers protect people.

A final Networker trick: they create the impression of being really busy. I know classic Networkers who have their friends believing that they are the busiest people on earth. They talk long and often about "getting together sometime" but can be the most slippery people to pin down for things that they don't want on their radar.

LEMON TRUISM: A Networker has time to do whatever a Networker wants to do.

They choose what goes on their radar, and they drop people and things off their radar at will. They can adjust their schedules at short notice, and can make time if they want to. They are not as busy as you might suppose, and have a toolbox full of ways of appearing to be committed and communicating while, in reality, they are stringing things along, holding their options open. When a Networker displaying Networker-weaknesses says, "I'll get back to you" it can mean, "I am waiting to see what my options are, and if something more interesting or useful to me doesn't come along, I'll get back to you."

Adding up your Weaknesses

It isn't always fun looking at our weaknesses. Sometimes they arise from character flaws, sometimes we are just not as disciplined as we should be, but often weaknesses are simply factors in our DNA that we have to acknowledge. Recognizing them is a good step towards growth. Better that we know our weaknesses than be the only person round the table who is oblivious to our blind spots.

So take a moment to review the weakness of LEMONs in this chapter and note those from each category that apply to you. Then count the number in each category and record them in the table below.

L	E	M	O	N

Total score on strengths – transfer to Your LEMON Profile in the Appendix.

Chapter 10
You say what you are

LEMON
speak

*Y*ou have no doubt heard the expression, "What you are speaks so loudly I cannot hear what you say." O that we understood this phrase better!

The truth is that everyone speaks in a context that includes culture, language, professional training and more. Perhaps the greatest context for the communication by leaders is how they are wired. Said another way, what leaders say is heavily influenced by their leadership type.

The implications are enormous. Unless we place the relevant LEMON filter on our ears and eyes when someone is speaking to us we will inevitably misunderstand what they are saying. Two people can say exactly the same words and honestly mean something different. Take the matter of what LEMONs consider to be work and how this translates to what they say.

"How is the project... is it complete?"
"It is just about done."

This is a simple statement, but what does "it is just about done" mean? Here are some possibilities (with dramatic license, of course):

Luminaries	I have considered it, thought through the ramifications, there are no logical reasons why it cannot be done, and someone is probably taking care of it. If it wasn't well under way already, someone would have told me.
Entrepreneurs	We have all of our ducks in a row, the right players are mostly on board, and we are nearing completion of a prototype, although there are, of course, still a few risks... but we can handle them.

Managers	The task is near to completion and I would put it above 90% complete. We have the processes, people and resources in place to get the other 10% done, and it will be finished in the near future.
Organizers	I already finished it [unspoken: to my 70% tolerance level].
Networkers	I have thought about a bunch of people who can almost definitely do it. I called several of them, got a few voicemails, but bumped into Jack, and he has a cousin who will definitely get it done. So it's as good as just about done.

Why is this? Are they all lying? How can it be that the answer to a simple question such as, "How is the project... is it done?" can yield such different results? Remember, each of the LEMONs sees a different reality. This is one reason why corporations have reports, financial statements and standard memorandum formats. When it comes to informal communications, personal interactions or, I am sorry to say, conversations with those in the less precise and the less accountable non-profit world, one has to especially hear what people say through the grid or lens of who they are. One needs the filters to translate from their LEMON type to yours.

Go with the communications flow

When you interact with someone, let the conversation take a natural flow with him or her taking the lead in the conversation. Observe the language clues, and this will tell you something about how they are wired. When interacting with a Networker there is a certain amount of early conversation that goes to talking about who they have met with recently, who is coming to town, who they spoke with on the phone, and who you have been in dialogue with of late. This marks out the fresh boundaries of their networking territory so that you know the boundaries of the network. (This can be for the good as in, "Look at all the possibilities for new connections!" or for the bad, "These are my trees in my network and I peed on them first.")

It works both ways. When you are leading the conversation what do you talk about? This will tell you something about how you are wired. Does the conversation plunge down the hole of your new opportunities, or all the things on which you have come to closure?

The LEMON Communication Matrix

Given your fresh understanding of LEMONs, it should not be too hard to figure out their patterns of communication. To get your juices flowing, consider the following table that has some broad generalizations about LEMON communications. Then we will dig into what each of the LEMONs says and hears, and provide some tips for communicating.

	Content	Media	Speed	Frequency
L	Ideas	Writing	Measured	Intermittent
E	Opportunities	Verbal Proposals	Fast	Frequent
M	Processes Policies	Writing Memos Meetings	Deliberate	Routine
O	Crisis Issues	Verbal Cellphone	Fast. Frantic	Immediately
N	Weaving	Verbal, whatever	Whatever it takes	In the moment

Luminary speak

You can tell a lot about who a leader is by the way in which they phrase their communications. The words of a LEMON are a window into their minds; they give us a glimpse as to how the person sees life. Observe the telltale words of Luminaries.

Luminaries say...	Luminaries don't say...
Here's the plan...	Is there a better plan?
I've got it all figured out.	Am I missing anything major?
Don't bother me with the details.	What pertinent details should I know?
Tell me everything about this tiny area.	What details can I afford to let go?
Who's on board with the plan, vision, dream?	Who do we need to make this happen?

Corking the Luminary pressure cooker

There is a story and a character or two behind each of the suggestions below. Luminaries tend to weigh in like 800-pound gorillas, and do so with the same intensity on any issue. It is not that they are always heavy handed (although this is sometimes true) but the ideas, which have been brewing in their pressure cooker, come out with force and intensity. So if you are a Luminary:

- Avoid the temptation to communicate continuously.
- Trade the machine gun for a rifle.
- Pre-think how you plan to interact with the organization; your communication causes waves.
- Channel your interactions to the points of highest payback.
- Avoid non-essential areas, recognizing that your ability/ tendency to have laser focus can be good and bad.
- Be careful to delineate tactics from strategies.
- New tactics will be interpreted as strategy de jour if you don't set the context clearly.
- Tone down the intensity.

- Do not frustrate the actions of others by claiming they are in violation of principles you hold intuitively but have not documented and discussed.

LEMON TRUISM: Try to avoid killing 1 ounce problems with 10 pound hammers.

The fact is, Luminaries like dialogue and debate. The problem is that when Luminaries present ideas they come across as being long-held, thought through, and unswerving. The reality is that the idea might have just popped into their minds en route to the coffee machine. If a Luminary does not tone down the presentation, it either kills further contributions or sends the organization on a wild goose chase. One of my clients was the President of a 1,000 person company. He lamented that when he "casually mentioned a new product idea" to a colleague he would bump into them a few weeks later and find that a new product team had been formed. There was obviously something in the conviction of his conversation that made the hearer feel that this was well thought through, and worth acting on. (Needless to say, the organization was crippled by product overload.)

What Luminaries hear

How often have we been frustrated in communications when dealing with friends or family? Many of the breakdowns in relationship arise from failures in communication. A key reason for this is that we do not fully grasp the radical differences in communication patterns between different types of people. Just how does a Luminary—or any other of the LEMONs for that matter—hear things?

If we want any LEMON to remember what we say, then we should communicate in their LEMON language. This means figuring out what they hear and don't hear. Do not make the mistake of assuming that what you would want to hear is what they would want to hear unless you are sure that they are wired the same way as you. I have watched entire conversations take place between people who have worked in the same organization for twenty years, and they missed each other in the communications because they did not adjust their way of speaking. The results were disastrous.

Luminaries hear...	They tend not to hear...
I like your ideas; I buy into your vision.	I don't like you.
I do/don't align with your intellectual constructs.	I am not totally comfortable with where are going.
[From their own fertile minds they hear] With a few adjustments the ideas or plans of others can be recast in terms of my plan.	These people don't really want to be subsumed by my vision.
I will be joining you!	I might have some reservations about joining you and am thinking it over.
There are endless possibilities.	There are limited resources.

Let's unpack this for a moment. Because Luminaries are prone to ideas, they filter what they hear to ascertain the degree of alignment with their own mental framework. Assume for a moment that you share something with them and it is consistent with how they see the world: they will hear the agreement, but may not notice the body language and chemistry (or lack thereof) that indicates that you do not plan to align yourself with them. They may not hear that you are not totally comfortable.

An area that Luminaries usually don't like to hear about is resource constraints. My wife once asked me, "Can you ever have too much vision?" I thought the question was a joke. Was she serious? How can you have too much vision? It took me a few years to figure out that I could drown my people in vision; that too much vision was indeed possible if there were not the resources to implement the vision. This is obvious to others; this is not so obvious to Luminaries who somehow believe that ingenuity will create its own resources.

So what do you do if you are trying to communicate with a Luminary? As with any of the LEMONs, one has to tailor one's communication to their leadership DNA if one is to maximize the likelihood of being heard. Here are some tips for communicating with Luminaries.

- Quicker is usually better. You don't have to fill in every blank for them to hear you.
- Set a time, if possible, when you can get their full attention. They are easily distracted, so you could lose your agenda in the flurry of new ideas that emanate from the meeting.
- Shorter is normally sweeter, unless they happen to zone in on a particular topic, in which case they could go deeper.
- Have the detail, but don't lead with it. Paint the broad outline, give them the edges of the puzzle, then fill in some of the details. Stated another way, set the context for what you are saying before you jump into the detail until asked.
- Make sure your logic hangs together. Don't confuse half-details with half-logic.
- Half-baked ideas can be dead-on-arrival, unless you are asking them for thinking help. Try to think through the implications of our proposal before presenting it.
- Don't start your responses to their "brilliant" ideas with "But," "No," or "In your dreams…"
- Link things back to their strategies so that they can be sure it is integrated into the broader context. You may think a Luminary is fighting you on the specifics of something when they are actually probing to ensure that you understand the context or bigger picture.

Entrepreneur-speak

The exact way in which an Entrepreneur communicates will vary with the stage of the development of their opportunity or business. During the early stages they are testing the veracity of ideas, whether there is a market, how the product or service needs to be tweaked, and what needs to be changed to reduce risk. The extent to which they do their homework will depend on some other factors, such as training, their formal field of study, and the modus operandi of their field.

If they are not specifically in business, they still go through similar sets of activities. Someone starting a school, government initiative or a non-profit will spend time building different types of capital, such as relational and political capital, and their communication will similarly reflect their gathering, trying on mentally, and testing with others.

When they are looking for external funding (in cases where they need this) they are in sales mode about the prospects of the corporation. When dealing with internal matters they are bottom-line oriented with an eye on how investors would view the internal workings of the company.

Allowing for these and other differences to be a factor during the various stages of the corporate lifecycle, let's take a look at some general Entrepreneur communication patterns.

Entrepreneurs say...	Entrepreneurs don't say...
Here's the deal...	Did you have something different in mind?
This is a great opportunity...	I am not sure if it will fly.
Are you on board?	Take a while to think about this.
We need some early wins...	What are the long-term implications of these early wins?
Let's get a team to make something happen...	Let's develop a detailed plan and properly allocate the right resources to the opportunity.

Here are some tips for Entrepreneurs when communicating with non-E's.

- Don't over-simplify: where there is complexity, acknowledge it and communicate how you are taking it into account.

- Share that you understand the need for permanent infrastructure at the right time; invite input from the Managers who can give your opportunity legs.
- Acknowledge the issues and communicate your risk mitigation strategies.
- Invite participation from the Networkers who can place relational kindling under your new fire.

When speaking with an Entrepreneur…

- Get to the punch line quickly.
- Be excited or passionate: demonstrate belief.
- Do not be pedestrian.
- Prove that you have skin in the game.
- Share their risk.

Each of us has a bit of every slice of the LEMON. Some years ago when pursuing clients was a daily routine, I often found myself saying to my team, "Here's the deal…" It took a conscious effort to change my opening line, but I had to do so because it left little room for a different look at the deal. And because Entrepreneurs are generally optimists, I heard myself and others saying, "This is a great opportunity!" Soon I learned to develop Opportunity Filters to discern the great from the not-so-great.

The truth and nothing but the truth

Blowing smoke at Managers is a bad communication strategy; they are born with sensitive smoke detectors. They may be amused by the stories of Luminaries, Entrepreneurs and Networkers, but they generally don't buy them. Managers want the truth. Consequently, their stories can be too factual for other LEMONs—not enough color and imagination. A Manager's story often sounds better when re-told by a Networker unless the Manager can deadpan the story in a way that is funny because it is so straight.

Managers say...	Managers don't say...
Having considered the alternatives...	I just thought of something wild...
We have a deliberate approach...	Let's just wing it and see what happens...
Good things come to those who prepare...	Good things just come.
This is what could go wrong...	This is a piece of cake!
The events unfolded as follows:	Do you want to hear the funniest story in the world?

Having said this, there are Managers who just wing it. They are, however, the exception.

Managers who are choosing a path of communication must take their target audience into account. The chances are that you will often be communicating with LE-ONs who don't care as much about some of the things that bother you. Some pointers for Managers:

- Lead with sound bites; follow with the facts.
- Include quick—emphasis on the quick—stories and word pictures in your delivery.
- Make the LE-ONs feel the pain (of not doing Manager things), painlessly.
- Inject humor into the communication where possible or relevant.
- Limit your time on issues.
- Watch the body language of your audience for glazing. If you see the screen saver go on, it is time to wrap it up.

When communicating with Managers, make sure that you understand the weight of their concerns. If you are a non-Manager, be sure to invite their participation and the value they can add early enough in the process. Managers are not wild about getting pulled in at the last minute to "do a bit of Quality Assurance" and "make sure that the numbers are right." While some corporations use them to rubber stamp done deals, this is a poor use of the strengths of a Manager.

- Lead with facts.
- Demonstrate due process.
- Show that you have considered various options.
- Prove that risk has been considered and mitigated.
- Dial down the hysteria.

Managers want to know that there is heart in an idea, a passion behind the proposal. But they want the passion in support of truth, so make sure that you build a track record of substantiated facts in your communications with a Manager. If you are prone to telling stories, make sure that the belief index of your Manager is high enough before you regale him or her with yet another exploit.

Managers lose the thread in communication when it is too random. Some other leaders are Masters of Random and use it as a tactic to shake the more serial processors off their trail.

Up close and personal

If you want to make sense to an Organizer you need to keep to the near-term, the issues and action items, and sometimes the personal. It's not that they don't like details: they do. But they have to be details about real people with real issues and real solutions, not theories about global warming and its impact on the Gross Domestic Product of Mars.

Organizers say...	Organizers don't say...
Houston, the engine's on fire.	In my opinion, and I say this before having conducted serious research, a heating challenge might develop in the near future.
This isn't working.	There are a few wrinkles that I am sure we can all just live with.
What do we have to do today?	Tell me your long-range plan.
...so I just did it.	...so I formed a committee.

Organizers are not usually long on formal communications. They have little regard for fluff and formality, particularly when it is disconnected from the facts as they see them. Consequently, Organizers are loath to add the padding that the corporation might expect. To them, email or voicemail is a welcomed relief from formal corporate Memoranda. They pride themselves on being tactical and practical. This does not always help them in communicating with others, however.

So what are the things that an Organizer can do when communicating with the LEM-Ns? Here are some suggestions:

- Acknowledge the "strategic" context before jumping into "To Do's." When speaking to LEMs say, "I know you have a Master Plan, and…"
- Put some sort of rating scale on the fire alarms. "This is a two alarm fire—not everyone will be burned all at once." Organizers function in the realm of the immediate, so when something comes up, they tend to respond to it right away, unless they are in overload, in which case they stuff it in a box and ignore it. They do not have the same filtering mechanisms of Managers. So if you are an Organizer, ask yourself whether your urgent items have the same level of urgency to others.
- Ask questions to gauge how others see a situation before rushing to action. You might say, "I see this as urgent, but how do you see it?"
- Dial down emotionally loaded speech such as, "This will never work…" and "He is a disaster…" and the Organizer's favorite, "I have a real integrity issue with this." This is a challenge for the Organizer because they make progress by getting others to share their sense of the immediate. And this is often exactly what is needed… but not always. Now is not always right.

A hint for non-O's: When you hear an Organizer say, "That sounds good, but it is not going to work," then you have to learn to ask a series of follow-on questions that help uncover the crux of the matter. Continue this process until the Organizer feels genuinely heard, then you probably have the issues on the table, whether you agree with them or not. So when you speak to O's:

- Keep a single thread in the conversation. This will help them feel they have been heard.
- Work towards action items. This honors the Organizer's need to have some things come to closure.
- Test whether they buy into what you are saying. Although Organizers may have fewer opinions on philosophy, they still need to concur, so taking a pause to check their level of alignment is important. Give them space to ponder and opine.
- Give them time to think about the issues and practical approaches. Organizers often know intuitively that there is an issue, but they may need time to define exactly what their concerns are. Do not steamroll them.
- Make sure they know you have considered the people issues. Organizers often care about the underdog and are attuned to personal ramifications of change. If you want an Organizer to feel comfortable, make sure that they know that you have considered the people aspects – or ask her to help you figure them out.
- Don't throw such a wide visionary net that the practical application is impossible to fathom. The lights in an Organizer's eyes will dim if the tangible gets swallowed by the intangible. Keep verbs in your sentences when speaking with an Organizer.

Networker-speak

When driving along farm roads you inevitably come to gates. Someone has to get out of the car and open the gate; then someone has to wait until the car has passed through and close the gate again. Networkers are good at opening gates, but not so good at closing them. They initiate communications with lots of people; they are not as good at closing the communications. They therefore leave lots of loose ends unless they are in hot pursuit of a specific objective. Stated another way, when they need information they are dogged. When they owe others a response, they are elusive.

Networkers say...	Networkers don't say...
Let's get together sometime!	When, where, why.
I totally love spending time with you.	I could spend time with most people who still mist up a mirror.
You are awesome!	Just like everyone else.
I want to get you together with Joe...	By the way, Susie, Jim and Chuck will be there too, for reasons that will be clear to no one but me.
She is one of my closest friends...	Along with 99 other best friends.

My wife, Lyn, says, "People like people who make them feel good about themselves." Networkers have the knack of doing this, and meaning it while they do so. People therefore love being around a Networker. They keep conversation flowing, and give life an easy flow. If the organization were a car, the Networker would be the grease that keeps things lubricated. Their ability to affirm can smooth over many tough situations. (Perhaps the Entrepreneur would be the engine, the Manager the chassis/structure, the Organizer the fuel system or electronics, and the Luminary the headlights.)

I hear like a...	L	E	M	O	N

Being a Networker gives you advantages and responsibilities in your communications. You are comfortable speaking with people, you seldom run out of things to say, and people warm to you. The flipside is that you know what people want to hear. This creates the danger that you say what you intuit people will want to hear. This, if left unchecked, can blunt your grasp of things and create a world where perceptions are more important than things.

When listening as an Networker, make sure you don't filter what people say to match what you have for sale in your shop window.

There are a few practical communication hints for an Networker:

- Acknowledge where you do not have the facts. Don't state as a fact that which you are only partly sure of; it will kill your credibility.
- Be clear about what is clear; be specific about what is open-ended. Not everyone has the same tolerance for ambiguity as you do.
- Recognize where you are avoiding tough communications, and grab the bull by the horns.
- Close the farm gates: sit down at the end of each week and make a note of those whom you have left dangling. Close the communication loop where you can.

I talk like a...		L	E	M	O	N

Affirming LEMONs

"Get not your friends by bare compliments, but by giving them sensible tokens of your love." (Socrates, 469 BC - 399 BC)

"The happy phrasing of a compliment is one of the rarest of human gifts, and the happy delivery of it another." (Mark Twain)

"I have yet to find the man, however exalted his station, who did not do better work and put forth greater effort under a spirit of approval than under a spirit of criticism." (Charles M. Schwab)

It is obvious that we all like to receive a compliment. Less obvious is that LEMONs like to receive affirmation in different ways. Think back on the compliments you have received in your lifetime: which ones stuck in your psyche? What does this tell you about what you value, and how you are wired? So the question is, "How should you affirm each of the LEMONs so that they feel most valued for who they are?"

We often send verbal cues so that others will communicate back to us the things we would like to hear. Even the way we say things is an indication of how we would like others to communicate to us. Many people don't like to play the mutual verbal back scratching game. When someone does this to me I am reminded of the saying, "Flattery is disguised hostility." Nonetheless, we should listen to what people offer as praise: it will give us insights into which LEMON they are. We should also note where they struggle to affirm others, as it will tell us where they struggle to feel good about themselves.

Here is a quick summary of things LEMONs like to hear.

Luminaries	Entrepreneurs	Managers	Organizers	Networkers
You have the best insights in this area of anyone I know.	You can make a go of anything.	You run a tight ship… so efficient.	You are a no-nonsense, make it happen person.	I like you… we all like you!

"If I can put one touch of rosy sunset into the life of any man or woman, I shall feel that I have worked with God." (G. K. Chesterton)

Go to Your LEMON Profile in the Appendix and make a note of how you like to be affirmed.

I like to be complimented for…	Ideas	Moving and shaking	Efficiency	Action	Being likeable

Affirming LEMONs is one thing: confronting them is another matter entirely.

Chapter 11
LEMONs in flight

*I*nsecurity leads to some combination of rejection and rebellion.

If you are one of the many who did not arrive on earth as an adult there is some chance that you grew up with parents and other authority figures who were not perfect role models. This results in insecurity at some level. Depending on the strength of your character you will have responded to this lack with some combination of two things: rejection and rebellion. For all of us, when criticism, pressure and opposition come our way we can either feel dejected or antagonistic, or both. Beyond these baseline tendencies lies a set of more specific patterns for each LEMON, and it may help to know the likely outcome when you find that your book of the month club has inadvertently picked *Who Squeezed my LEMON?*

Putting the LEMON squeeze on people

The reason we do things in a particular way is, for the most part, because we think our way is right. Absent some sinister motive, we develop patterns of doing things, and when these patterns are challenged we respond negatively. Given the many different types of people in the world there is a strong chance that people don't see things the way you do. I am more and more convinced that when I react strongly to someone else's take on things—that is, when I think they are dead wrong—it is not because of some irrefutable truth that I have and they don't. The real reason is this: they are a different LEMON type.

My tendency is to put the LEMON squeeze on people and argue for the rightness of my position. Sometimes I win the battle. They leave my home or my office nodding their heads. "You are right; I just didn't see it that way." A week or two later, however, they are back to where they started unless what I said actually contained some core truth that went beyond my usual devious persuasiveness. How many times have I burned someone at an intellectual or emotional stake because I failed to understand how he or she was put together? How many times have I squeezed my slice of the LEMON on them instead of becoming one of them?

Becoming one of... them!

"Become one of them? You must be joking! When the squeeze is on I will become more like me—more of an N... Give me an N! Give me an E! Give me a T!"

The problem with the idea of becoming more like others is that it swims against the stream of my presumed right to independence. "I gotta be me!"

> **LEMON TRUISM: We were made for interdependence, not independence. Even our leadership is designed to be as part of a team.**

The Western movies had it wrong—King Arthur had it closer to the truth. Leadership does not exist in a vacuum. While there is a leader among equals, this is more a matter of function than of hierarchy. When we fathom this truth, then the notion of becoming like the other slices of the LEMON in order to hear, understand, weigh and learn is not so hard.

LEMONs in crisis

We would avoid the crisis that faces many leaders if we grasped this reality that we are inter-dependent leaders who function best when related to other gifted people. The tendency in the United States of America is to aggrandize leaders during the courtship and honeymoon stages, and slaughter them in a crisis. Imagine if we were circumspect about leaders during the honeymoon stage and supportive in a crisis. (And think of all the bad TV commentators we could avert.)

There are a number of jobs that carry a lifespan of 18 months—CIO, CMO and pastor—just like an iPod battery or computer memory. There are all sorts of reasons posited for this, but my belief is that leaders have about eighteen months of grace and then the trouble begins if they have failed to adapt the Operating Model of the organization to their LEMON type. This is a challenge because most organizations hire people who will not rock the boat. The new leader figures it is smart to buy a little time before they make drastic changes. After a quarter or two they rearrange the furniture. Then they rearrange some people and restructure the organization so that it has labels and departments that are more comfortable to the leader. The vast majority of leaders fail to completely overhaul the Operating Model in order to align it with their LEMON type. A Networker cannot run an operation constructed around a founding Luminary. A Manager cannot deliver the goods using an organization structured for a Networker.

Back to the glorifying of new leaders: the truth is we don't totally idolize them during the honeymoon stage because, somewhere in a back room, custodians of the way things have always been done are ardently protecting the old modus operandi. The dualism is that we smile in public and dig in our heels in private.

> **LEMON TRUISM: If you fail to align the Operating Model to your leadership type in your first two years in office, it's just a matter of time until the organization rejects your leadership.**

The lifespan of leaders is short. We should put a circle of complementary LEMONs in place as soon as someone is hired so that, when the new leader loses his grip, there is a safety net in place to ensure that it isn't fatal.

Fight, flight, wellness patterns

It is not helpful to respond with a bleeding heart to every criticism that comes our way. Neither is it productive to deflect what could be useful input. LEMONs have the usual ways of responding to "input" or "feedback" as people like to call it, but we each have some very specific things unique to our wiring. Stored within our leadership DNA are patterns for getting through the onslaughts that inevitably come. Unfortunately not all of our reactions are helpful. In many cases they will cause us to deepen the hole we are in. For the most part, our dominant wiring as a LEMON can become a weakness if we fail to grow in areas less comfortable for us.

Let's just say you are a LEMON and there are people out there who hope to improve your leadership capabilities. You can fight them, flee them, or work with them. It may be helpful to see these common patterns laid out in a grid. The "fight" scenarios are the first volleys we have to stave off the attackers. These normally precede the flight options and kick in while we still think we have a chance of surviving. The "flight" responses are those that we have when we deal with a situation by leaving. They can be the last comment we have over our shoulder as we walk out the door. The more sane responses of a secure leader are in the "Wellness" column.

Here's your game plan if you are a Luminary.

Type	Fight	Flight	Wellness
L	Baffle the organization with intellect.	Explain clearly why the people you were leading were messed up, not advanced enough for your thought leadership.	Embrace the situation as a growth opportunity where they can add to your intellectual and personal assets.

As a good fighting Luminary your first response to criticism—constructive or otherwise—is to strew even more ideas in the path of would be assailants. Your opponents will have to pick their way through the obstacle course of new strategies and ideas. If you throw out 10 good ideas, there should be one or two good ones that they have to at least pause to consider, otherwise they will look like they are simply out to get you. This will give you the breathing room to not have to consider their input seriously.

If you are losing the battle and are about to be labeled functionally useless, then it might be a good time to flee. Be sure to explain to yourself and anyone else who will listen that the people you were leading were not smart enough to appreciate your leadership. If you are a thought leader—a legend in your own mind—then the vacant smiles on their faces as you leave will prove that you were simply too advanced for them.

The "wellness" response—responding in a whole manner to the input being offered—has some similar attributes across the LEMONs. A healthy understanding of who we are includes a level of comfort with who we are not, which in turn creates mental and emotional space for growth.

So if you are a healthy Luminary and realize you are not the only ornament on the Christmas tree, you will embrace the opportunities to grow your personal vault of intellectual assets, your emotional IQ, your life tools, or your spiritual capital.

As an Entrepreneur you can develop (and perhaps package and sell) your own set of diversionary tactics. Your ability to bounce from one opportunity to the next should be used to fend off those who want to press in and help you grow. When one opportunity is questioned as a "case in point" to get you to focus on weaknesses, simply throw three better opportunities on the table, some of which require urgent attention. This sucks up the energies of your antagonists, or at least provides you with an excuse to leave the uncomfortable dialogue and go out to chase deals.

Type	Fight	Flight	Wellness
E	Create a new initiative – throw more heat at the problem.	Start something new somewhere else. Get a better offer.	See "a new me" as the new opportunity, and embrace the change.

If this doesn't work and you couldn't be bothered with growing, take off and start a new business. You will get praised for your new ideas, so it is natural to say, "That didn't work out; every good Entrepreneur has a few failed attempts, and I have seven new ideas that are even better."

You may be an Entrepreneur who realizes that you do not have the whole package when it comes to leadership capabilities, and you cope with difficulties by becoming your own next opportunity. Starting up "the new me" becomes an Entrepreneurial endeavor, and your strength works in your favor.

Where people have the audacity to question your well thought-through Manager ways, there is a simple answer: create more work, keep them busy, take away their spare time, don't allow them to sit around and contemplate strategies to fix Mr. Manager.

Type	Fight	Flight	Wellness
M	Tighten the screws, institute new processes and controls.	Point out the immaturity of the organization to handle a leader of his/her ilk, and move on.	Loosen up to other styles of leadership. Build a surrounding organization with complementary gifts.

If the organization doesn't buy this diversion, as a "mature manager" you may conclude that the corporation simply does not have the maturity to deal with your advanced managerial ways. So leave. (PS: I have seen quite a few situations where people got fired or forced out of organizations mainly because they were high on the obnoxious scale, but when you hear their version of things, the organization was not ready for their vast store of managerialness.)

If you are a healthy Manager, loosen up, surround yourself with people who represent other slices of the LEMON, and don't kill your colleagues with the Operations Manual. Then deliberately build your team to cover other facets of leadership. Avoid just hiring other Managers to do your bidding.

While Luminaries use ideas to fend off others, Entrepreneurs use new Opportunities as a red herring, and Managers squeeze out opposition through new procedures, you as an Organizer can fight fire with fire. If people want you to become "more corporate" the first thing to do is start a new fire, and make sure you are the only one who knows where the fire extinguisher is. This will prove why you are indispensable. Or, if you have the leeway, launch a new flurry of activity. The goal as usual: distract the vultures and consume the energy of the medics.

Type	Fight	Flight	Wellness
O	Launch a new event or find a more compelling issue that distracts the vultures and consumes the medics.	Find a new cause, usually somewhere else.	Learn that 'strategy' and 'opening new windows' is as valuable as nose-down 'coming to closure.'

If you decide not to grow with the organization, consider taking your fire fighting skills to a new venue. In the early days the chaos of your current situation fed your identity. As things became more institutionalized you faced an identity challenge: stay and be constructive, or move on. In a worst case scenario you could stay and throw hand grenades in the corporate pond.

There is another identity-preserving mechanism for Organizers that will interest you. I call it the Organizer Kamikaze Syndrome. It is 11h45 and the deadline is 12h00; or it is two days before they leave on vacation; it is three feet from the edge of the cliff, and the avid Organizer decides to turn things up a notch. Rather than back away from the brink, they go Kamikaze. Instead of executing a graceful transition or reigning in their mount, they label themselves "Willing" and spur the horse as they gallop towards the cliff, then leap off the edge and impale themselves on the stake called "Thankless Impossibilities." Their tombstone reads, "Here lies a spent Organizer... you'll be sorry when I am gone."

The wellness response of an Organizer involves a deliberate decision to grow in their secondary LEMON type. I often get asked, "What is the growth path for an Organizer?" The bigger question is whether the Organizer wants a growth path. Sure, we all want to grow, but the high level of intuition coupled with a disdain for the overly structured can lead an Organizer into being stuck as an Organizer. So the first key to a wellness response is being open to rounding out who you are by embracing the other slices of the LEMON.

If you are a Networker and want to confound your opponents, then practice deliberate relational confusion. Throw a few more names in the ring, weave them together, add a few second cousins, and pretty soon everyone will know they cannot do without your spider web, nor the spider. Or they would have forgotten what they were challenging you about.

Type	Fight	Flight	Wellness
N	Throw an impressive array of new relationships into the mix; deliberate relational confusion.	Find a new network somewhere else that really appreciates your talents and promises to free you up from grunt work.	Learn to submit the vagaries of weaving/ schmoozing to the discipline of process... Let others in on the network (i.e., give up fierce control of the Rolodex).

Another technique is to charm people. This too will divert them. Make your fight look like a love fest. Yet another mechanism you can use is to admit your faults—not the real one, just the ones that people will feel sorry for—and hope to get sympathy.

If these don't work, you may need to pack up your Rolodex and move on to a situation where you don't have to conform too much, and where you are free to just schmooze. Or you can respond in wellness, give up the fierce control of your Rolodex, and submit yourself to the disciplines of a well rounded organization. Get some real friends, not just a long list of acquaintances.

LEMON TRUISM: Leadership is important, but it is not everything.

For all LEMONs, lighten up, step back from yourself, give the people whom you are leading a bit more credit, and don't take yourself so seriously. This is pretty much the key to responding in a holistic way to the inevitable critique that comes with the job. I remember hearing Herb Morris say that one of the keys to successful negotiating is "caring, but not too much." I have had more than one earnest person discourse about why LEMON may not be such a good name because it implies leaders may have some faults. Hello? All leaders have plenty of faults. In fact, one of the biggest faults we have is that we take ourselves too seriously. A friend relayed his story to me about how, when he was an earnest young pastor, he committed a serious social faux pas during a funeral service for a Chinese family. It seemed none of his zealous preaching could do anything to capture the attention of the guests who weren't part of his usual congregation, so he was all the more keen to get through to them. The guests talked loudly among themselves, taking no notice of him while he tried to deliver his deliberately constructed sermon. Then he spotted this large red button on the pulpit and, in slow motion, his arm took on impulses of its own, moved away from his body, and hit the button. The still open casket proceeded down the conveyor belt to the awaiting crematorium. The only problem was that this was a burial. The guests went into pandemonium. Fortunately the open lid got stuck in the jaws of the conveyor and an army of Asians swarmed around trying to save the deceased from the inevitable fire. Hours later as my friend asked God, "Why did this happen?" the answer seemed to come. "To teach you not to take yourself too seriously." Sometimes leaders are more serious about themselves than God is. With an appropriate dose of self deprecation, let's examine the normal patterns of LEMONs being squeezed.

Avoidable crises

If you are involved in a fairly organic organization such as a not-for-profit charity, watch out for the tendency to assign your internal operations the status of The 10 Commandments. The memorializing of your mundane modus operandi can cause unnecessary conflict.

If you are the leader of an organization and the keeper of the corporate story there is a deeper danger. You may be holding convictions that are not written down and yet they govern everyday affairs in your organization. Others experience a crisis when they encounter these operating assumptions that are like uncharted rocks below the surface of the water. This results in the flight of leaders because there is no sane path to peace, and the tension of not knowing when the next subterranean rock will gash a hole in their leadership is too risky.

My LEMON Profile

	L	E	M	O	N
I fight like a...	L	E	M	O	N
I take flight like a...	L	E	M	O	N
I respond well like a...	L	E	M	O	N

Record your observations in Your LEMON Profile.

This raises the topic of "Corporate LEMONs" — the dynamics of putting lots of LEMONs together. It doesn't always give you lemonade.

Chapter 12
Corporate LEMONs

I am not a corporate LEMON. You may be saying this if you are a running your own business, minding your own store, or shaping your own household. Chances are, you are a still a corporate LEMON.

You may have found the frequent references to corporations, organizations and companies strange. Yet each of us has a context in which we exercise our leadership. Whether you are one person at a desk, in a repair truck or in a classroom, you are still a LEMON and interact with other LEMONs constantly.

Plural LEMONship

Villages have elders who drive for consensus. Presbyterians have elder boards. Synagogues have had elders for centuries. Plural leadership is not uncommon. Yet recently someone explained to me that their breakdown in decision-making came about because three people were working together in making decisions. "It works for the Trinity," I told him. In the USA there is a steady flow of mind food that says the leader is an individual. This is reinforced with trite sayings about "someone has to call the shots," "the buck stops here" and, in the Absolut Husky slogan, "If you're not the lead dog the view never changes." Tall, quiet, little discussion, bold decisions made by one person, (usually a man) with admiring onlookers... good for Westerns, bad for life. Some other cultures have a greater appreciation for team leadership.

The more society moves into knowledge work the less the single leader idea is valid. Anyone with information or insight can make a contribution. Experience can produce character and wisdom, but contributions from a rich array of sources are crucial. In today's complex organization, leaders seldom stand alone. A chief executive is surrounded by a variety of shades of presidents and vice presidents that complement her wiring. Board members should likewise reflect the LEMON spectrum.

To be effective in plural leadership one has to understand several things:
- There is a difference between position and influence.
- There is an authority of influence that accrues to leaders who consistently exercises capable leadership with character.
- One can have equality of value and difference of function.

LEMON TRUISM: The best teams are those comprised of strong leaders with definite and distinctive abilities representing the entire LEMON spectrum, and having a code of leadership that honors each other and recognizes the calling of one to be a leader among equals.

Lead LEMONs carry weight

We have established that teams are good. The complexion and function of teams is, however, dramatically affected by the profile of the primary leader. The leadership type of the recognized leader tints the whole look-and-feel of the team, even when there is a leader among equals. Unless the leader deliberately offsets his or her own type, they will tend to build a team of people who are like them or are directly complementary to them in a non-threatening way. So Managers may stack the team with people who comply with their view of the world. They may even exclude other leadership types from the "inner circle." If the leader is blind to this, then the excluded leaders will re-group to set up a counter balance. This will also be counter productive, not because the alternate perspective in not right, but because meeting time is spent sharing alternative viewpoints or creating what are perceived by the outer circle to be "balancing strategies" that detract from the central direction. There is leakage of alignment and dilution of focus. If the primary leader creates the context where there is open sharing and appreciation for differences in leadership types, one can avoid the tyranny of the minority. It is the job of the leading LEMON to not just make space for all LEMONs at the table, but to help each function to the maximum, given the way they are wired.

When an extreme Luminary leads the team it becomes a marketplace of ideas where thoughts are the stock-in-trade. Debate is welcomed, opinions are considered, and broad solutions to long-term matters are frequently aired. The Luminary likes the interchange with bright minded leaders who can think along with the best of them. The hothouse of intellectual interchange will hopefully result in a focus on the right things. If the ideas are right, the results will be good. What may be going on in the back of the minds of the remaining –EMONs?

- E: Just give me an opportunity that I can break off from the idea iceberg and flow with.
- M: How can we get some boundaries around the thinking so that it can be translated into more predictable things with plans, budgets, and reporting so that others in the organization can get on with their lives?
- O: A verb. Please, someone give me a verb.
- N: This sounds good, but I wonder how many others out there are thinking this stuff? Are other organizations already ahead of the game, have we thought about working with them; can we get some external validation?

When an extreme Entrepreneur is leading the team it develops the feel of a locker room, not a boardroom. Idea sifting quickly gives way to opportunity selection. The underlying urgent question is, "What have we accomplished this week, this month?" There is a penchant for focus, narrowing down options, choosing a few things that can be done well, or first, or cheaper, or better. And what may be going through the minds of the L-MONs?

- L: Are we missing the bigger picture? Do we have the right strategic context? Will we gain in the near-term and lose in the long-term?
- M: Will we sacrifice long-term infrastructure development on the altar of quarterly profits? Will we actually build an organization or simply be ambulance chasers?

- **O**: This is cool, but are we ignoring some of the obvious issues? Are we paying enough attention to the people and their needs?
- **N**: Do I really have something to sell yet? Is it what the customers want? Is it as good as we have convinced ourselves it is?

When an extreme Manager leads the team the meetings feel ordered, measured and civil. Those who comply with reporting processes and meeting protocol get on well and bumps in the road on results are tolerated, probably even expected. The (fewer) good ideas that are kicked around should still be in the boundaries of the field and according to the unwritten rules of corporate custom. Things should not only be orderly, but they should appear to be orderly. And what might the LEMONs be thinking?

- **L**: I wonder how many seconds a raw, unpackaged fresh thought would last in this meeting?
- **E**: Do you think they would notice if I started a new division / office / competitive company and kicked their butts?
- **O**: (I hate meetings.) Has anyone noticed that our results are not quite what the reports say they are? Does anyone know that we have issues? These reports are pretty, on time, and dense… but they don't tell the real story.
- **N**: Maybe if I smile, agree that we need to tighten procedures, and eat a little managerial dirt, I can excuse myself and go and see a customer.

There was a ton of analysis that went into the well documented transition from Reg Jones to Jack Welch at General Electric. I believe that Jack Welch was successful in filling Jones's shoes because he knew, perhaps instinctively, that he had to change the Operating Model of GE to fit with his own leadership DNA. Had he not done so, he would have been a David in a Saul's armor.

When an extreme Organizer (who is light on a secondary slice) is leading the team, things are energetic, unpredictable, sometimes organized, and often spontaneous. Meetings have a flavor of telling it like it is and getting closure mixed with concern for overlooked issues. There are periodic eruptions caused by the ferreting out of unresolved issues. There will be highs and lows. Bring your own fire extinguisher to the meeting. What is going through the minds of the other LEM-Ns?

- **L**: What is the big picture? Can this person articulate a strategy that will unite us?
- **E**: We have to build a business not just put out fires. We seem to be confusing activity and work.
- **M**: We have little regard for processes and procedures, planning and rigor. Will I have the leeway to build something that will last before getting jerked in another direction?
- **N**: This person makes me look like a long-term strategist. How does this series of short-term wins add up to an annual plan, let alone a business strategy? What does this look like to my customers? I love "the close" but we have to close the right things.

When an extreme Networker is leading the team things can seem congenial, country club-ish, friendly and connected. Depending on the Networker's support structure, there may be order in the meetings, but not in a restrictive way. There will be lots of stories about new people, meetings, possibilities and dreams. Things will be optimistic, if not precise. There could be a fair amount of name-dropping and "who spoke to whom" going on in the meeting. People will feel they are connecting at a heart level. If the Networkers, as is true for others, do not lean into some of their other strains, then their leadership may feel a bit like this to the other LEMO-s:

- **L**: We seem to be changing strategy frequently. Can't we stick with one clear strategy for a while? The leader (N) is too easily influenced by whoever crosses their path, and lots of this seems to be random.

- E: We don't seem to pin something down and run with it. There always seems to be another relational connection that is exciting and that replaces the one that fell off the radar.
- M: There is a lack of specifics, near absence of accountability, and an air of suspicion around all these great people and companies we have met.
- O: The probability of this turning into real results is low. All these relationships are great, but do they really care about us, and what's in it for us?

Leaders and their Operating Models

Writings of the mid-1990s told us that corporations had to build their Operating Model to deliver the essence of their best offer to customers.

- If you are known for the best products, then the entire organization must be built to create great products. Creativity, fresh thinking, and absence of restrictions are prized. Product is king.
- If the organization is known for efficiency, then the discipline of "operational excellence" is the order of the day. Things have to run like clockwork for organizations such as McDonalds and Federal Express. Process is king.
- The final group of companies is service-oriented, and the discipline is called "customer intimacy." The idea is to maximize one's share of each customer relationship; consequently one shapes the entire organization around nurturing long-term client relationships.

Implicit in this thinking is that one can have leaders who come and go as long as the modus operandi of the organization stays highly focused on delivering value in its own unique way. There are two challenges with this concept. First, there are more than three ways to create value. Second, it fails to recognize the leadership factor.

> **LEMON TRUISM: A new leader who fails to adapt the organization to their leadership type will fail.**

Many corporations—profit and non-profit—bring in a new leader with great expectations. If there is alignment between the leader's LEMON-type and the way in which the organization operates, good things can happen. Often, however, they hire someone who is "fresh" or "different" so that changes can be made. This is a gamble because several factors work against this scenario being successful:

- There is an entrenched way of doing things (usually guarded by people who like things the way they were), and this seeks to conform the new leader to the old Operating Model.
- The new leader often decides to wait before making major changes. This only reinforces item # 1.
- If the new leader elects to immediately start making changes but fails to legitimately conform the Operating Model to who they are, they are also in trouble.

The short lifespan of anyone from Chief Information Officers to Pastors is testimony to this fact: people don't mind talk of change, but when you mess with the Operating Model to which they have become accustomed, you are in trouble, and if you try to run an organization without molding the organization to your own LEMON DNA, you are in trouble. Beware of job postings that say, "We want a leader with vision…," and the fine print says, "but we don't want her to change the Operating Model." This is akin to them saying, "We don't mind where you are going, we just don't like the way you are planning to get there." Leaders lead out of their identity, so the "where to" and the "how" are an integral package.

Personal Reflection

With the possible exception of the family, organizations that have been in existence for a while tend to peel off the slices of LEMON that don't fit the mold. Has your leadership contributed to this phenomenon?

- Who are the LEMONs that I avoid having on my team?
- Where have I had an "issue" with someone in the past?
- How could I have interacted differently if I had understood their LEMON type?
- What can I do to restore missing slices of the organizational LEMON?

Chapter 13
Shaping the LEMON

*T*he second most loving thing I can do for someone is confront them about their weaknesses.

So said a friend when I asked him why he had been successful in avoiding leadership crises with the leaders he had developed over a period of 30 years. Few people relish the task of helping people recognize and overcome weaknesses. If our motivation is what is best for the person then our methods and commitment to action will be pure. There will be times, however, when a face-to-face, specific discussion is essential. Some matters require immediate redressing such as ethical violations, behavior that is detrimental to colleagues and departure from stated corporate or family values.

If you are leading an organization you should set the expectation during the getting to know you phase, which is usually an interview, for employees, that the giving and receiving of correction is normal. During orientation or relationship building phases when new team members hear the corporate story and learn the legends, share instances where Mr. Big, now the head of the Thus and So Department, really messed up and was helped to overcome the situation. Establish a climate where admitting mistakes and getting help is the norm.

A friend, Michael Louis, shared how he joined the family business as a third generation owner. While he was fresh on the job he noticed someone engaged in what he perceived as wasting corporate assets. He chastised the person. Michael's father, still the chairman of the Louis Group, corrected Michael for his disregard of people, and commended him for thinking like an owner. Mr. Louis expressed a twin culture of affirmation and correction.

> "Flatter me, and I may not believe you. Criticize me, and I may not like you. Ignore me, and I may not forgive you. Encourage me, and I will not forget you. Love me and I may be forced to love you."
> (William Arthur Ward)

Kill me with kindness

There are numerous ways of getting someone's attention about leadership or personal deficiencies. A full-on, no-holds-barred assault is seldom the right starting point. We would rather cut them slack, give them grace, and kill the bad traits with kindness. As the saying goes, "First the honey, and then the vinegar." And there is merit in this. I am grateful for the people who have affirmed the few good things I may have done as a young leader instead of picking on the ten areas that they knew needed improvement. I will not bore you with the blindingly obvious such as speaking about the person as they could be and not just as they are, affirming their positive attributes, finding the sources of insecurity that cause obnoxious behavior, filling the mental potholes that cause the leader's bicycle to lurch and careen… these are all good steps to take. Add to this the good counsel about escalating things properly from a quiet personal discussion to a more public and documented affair—there are other places to find such advice.

My focus in this chapter is to ask a few questions about how you would like to be challenged about your opportunities for growth. My second objective is to help you increase the likelihood of success when speaking correctively to someone in leadership.

LEMON TRUISM: Clear values on their own do not a good leader make.

Values

Every organization should document their true values and work through their practical implications. This is indeed motherhood and apple pie in theory. Distill the five or six things that set the tone for the corporate climate and are the guidelines for behavior. Write them on cards, etch them on glass and instill them in the corporate memory. Until values are articulated they are non-negotiable. When you write them down they are open to scrutiny and debate. When they exist in the Founder's head they are pieces of furniture that one stumbles into in the dark.

More importantly, have the entire organization involved in thinking through the implications of these values. So if one of the values is "Relationships" then chalk out the implications. "We will not speak negatively about people. We will hold each other to high standards of conduct because failures here will ultimately break down relationships. We will not do anything that would break down trust between colleagues, customers, etc." These are implications of values.

Nothing kills an organization quite so quickly as someone in leadership getting away with violating the corporate values. Compromise on this, and things begin to unravel. Have an early warning system in place and measure compliance with values. More than this, anticipate where leaders will have difficulties based on their LEMON type.

Foundational Principles

One day I woke up to realize that there was a tug of war going on in my company, and the reason was that key leaders did not share my view of how things worked. Our values had been defined and we had discussed their implications. But there was a set of principles more specific to the inner workings of the organization itself that I had never documented. Values are like the concrete slab of a house. Foundational principles are like the piers driven by pile drivers into the bedrock of core beliefs. They go a lot deeper. A lot is said about Values; very little is written about what I call "Foundational Principles."

Just as each individual has a worldview, so each organization has a philosophy of business. A religious organization may call it a philosophy of ministry. This is the fundamental set of assumptions about how the organization works. The Foundational Principles develop over time and are shaped by many things including hereditary, education and input from key influencers.

Just as one's worldview is held consciously or unconsciously, so foundational principles are there, whether they are articulated or not. If values are like furniture that one bumps into in the night, foundational principles are like landmines. The implications of violating a leader's or organization's Foundational Principles can be catastrophic because more people, resources, relationships and reputations are at stake.

Why is it that people do not articulate Foundational Principles? I can think of several reasons:

- Ignorance: people don't know about the concept. They think about values at the personal level but do not understand the organic nature of this living, breathing thing called a corporation (whether for profit or not-for-profit).
- Fear: founders fear that if they articulate foundational principles then they will be challenged, tweaked and morphed. So they would rather clean up after the land mines than expose their inner beliefs.
- Tradition: we have a way of doing things and that's the way it is. The implication is that you have to stick around for a long time towing the corporate line so that you can learn the unspoken rules. The hope is that if you can live long enough to learn them then you will have been inoculated and will no longer be a threat.
- Laziness: some leaders don't want to be bothered thinking them through.

This is all background to state this next truism:

LEMON TRUISM: If a key leader knows the corporation's Foundational Principles and chooses to ignore, run loose with, or violate them, then that leader must leave or step down from leadership.

Ask it like it is… the LEMON way

Assuming that your reason for confronting someone is redemptive and that you want a productive result from the interaction, begin by asking questions. Pause for a moment and consider the most esteemed leader that you know who, in your view, is a Luminary. Pick someone you respect highly. Let's say that the scenario is that they have been too harsh on the people in their department. Now imagine that it is your job to challenge or correct them. What questions would you ask each of the LEMONs that could help them come to their own right conclusions?

Asking questions may get you there and may also only delay the inevitable straightforward conversation. In speaking to LEMONs keep in mind that who they are is a key driver for what they hear.

- **Luminary** – gently unveil the facts, without insulting their intelligence. Let them get the thread of your implicational questioning, and anticipate the right conclusion.
- **Entrepreneur** – enthusiastic communication; recommend different opportunities, not ideas, policies, controls, etc. Paint the picture of a better opportunity that would come about if they behaved differently.
- **Manager** – appeal to something higher; draw them out of the minutia of the moment, and avoid getting bogged down in a swamp of emotions. Once the facts have been established, however, help them make a heart connection about the matter at hand.
- **Organizer** – give them personal time; afford them the processing opportunity to come to terms with something in their particular way.
- **Networker** – provoke them, cause them to think, but don't destroy the relationship. Challenge where they are, then extend mercy.

What about you? What is it that you are least likely to do in handling a difficult situation? Few of us relish conflict, but the way we avoid it says something about how we are predisposed. Once again, it depends on how you are wired. If you are a:

- **Luminary** – you will tend to straighten out their thinking and not address their specific behaviors. You will help them discover where their principles are faulty, but may not say, "Your behavior has really hurt me."
- **Entrepreneur** – you may tell them that they are getting in the way of corporate success. You may tell them where they are killing good opportunities, but you may not dig into the root cause behind the abhorrent behaviors.
- **Manager** – you may focus on the enforcement of the letter of the law rather than the heart of the matter. You may tackle the broken process and not see the broken person.
- **Organizer** – you may overstate the issue as you may be more interested in getting it off your chest than in remedying the situation. Your goal may be to let the steam out of your own pressure cooker, which makes you feel better, but actually just transfers the pressure to someone else.
- **Networker** – you may tend to avoid the confrontation altogether. Just believe the best, bury differences, and hope that all will still be well. Beware, however, that a layer of distance will come between the relationship. Keeping problems at arms length is keeping problems.

LEMONS can be pruned

In the world of agriculture you don't actually have to prune citrus trees in order to increase their fruitfulness. You can shape them. If this were only true about people we would not have to experience half the problems we do. Most fruit trees need to be pruned, however, and a wise farmer knows that less is the path to more. One can hope that, as the leader matures, he or she has developed self-pruning disciplines so that the weight of this does not fall on the corporation. There is always a measure of pruning that only comes through peers, mentors and organizations.

Regrettably, none of us are totally shaped or pruned the way we should be. The more we resist self-pruning and the disciplines of an organization, be it a family, a peer group or a corporation, the higher the probability that each of us will yield to "The Dark Side of LEMONs."

Chapter 14
The dark side of LEMONs

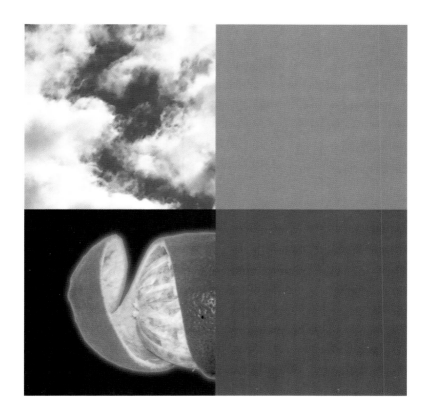

*B*y now you have a good sense of both the strengths and weaknesses of LEMONs. Having weaknesses is not a crime; recognizing them in advance helps us to overcome or at least mitigate them.

This is good information for us to have when we get out of bed on the right side, have eaten a balanced breakfast and are generally at peace with the world. But, if you are anything like me, every now and then one gets out of sorts and enters the world of the dark side of leadership. I have no great scientific reason for the Law of the Dark Side of LEMON Leadership, but have formulated it after countless observations of my own aberrant behavior. Then, having seen it in myself, I have also seen it in others. Here's the law:

LEMON TRUISM: On a good day I live the positive attributes of my primary LEMON slice. On a bad day I live out the negative attributes of my secondary LEMON slice.

Like any leader, I have a mix of the five slices of the LEMON. I am mostly a Luminary, and can be Entrepreneurial, a Networker, and Managerial. When starting up divisions or businesses I have been entrepreneurial. When building the Operating Model of clients and my own corporations I have been managerial. When selling, I have been a Networker. On some occasions, when the situation calls for it, I can be an Organizer for a short while. But mostly I am a Luminary. If you are a Luminary, it helps to know the field about which you think, perceive, dream and write. For me, it is often about how things work. While I am probably not a good Manager, I am Luminary about how organizations should be built. In recent years I have observed myself and noted that on a good day I display the bright side of a Luminary. I am creative, generate new ideas, I envision things that don't exist yet, and easily get people to warm to my ideas. On a bad day I am the Manager from Hell. Knowing the rules in the Office Policies and Procedures Manual (most of which I wrote, incidentally) better than my staff, I pick at their shortcomings, point out non-performance and become the self-appointed efficiency expert, watching with an eagle eye for any underperformance. What's worse, instead of just acknowledging that I should take some time out and stop being a fool, I justify my atrocity as being "attention to detail" or as "upholding the importance of some procedure or policy or principle." I act like The Master of the Myopic.

Watch out for your second slice

All of us LEMONs have a dark side to our leadership. This is generally a truism of human nature, and specifically a truism of leadership. No leader is without fault, so the occasional straying from the bright side is understandable and acceptable provided it is acknowledged.

LEMON TRUISM: Every LEMON has a dark side.

When we do not acknowledge our bad patterns then we can get into the realm of what some would call self-deception. Chuck Colson (a Luminary, in my view) says, "Humankind has an infinite capacity for self-deception." Being able to name our disingenuous behavior can save us from self-deception.

There is a level beyond the unthinking strolling across the line and the subtler self-deception: it is the matter of self-destruction. In some cases people exhibit an astounding ability to clutch defeat from the jaws of victory. There are many reasons for this, a common one being that we do not feel worthy of success, so we self-sabotage.

The question is, "How do we know when we are routinely crossing to the dark side?" The answer lies, in part, in having a good understanding of our secondary slices as they round out our leadership package. In particular, we must become familiar with the negative aspects of our particular leadership DNA so that we can avoid falling into its dark pit by default. In exploring each of these I will use the term "secondary LEMON" to refer to the secondary leadership type. (It doesn't matter too much what the primary type is in this instance.)

- A secondary Luminary will try to drown a situation in an endless stream of new ideas when what is needed is focus on a few things that actually work. Even in situations of serious impropriety they will try to pull the wool over the organization's eyes by substituting a new vision that renders past failures of no consequence. Think about the political, corporate or religious leaders who have committed moral wrongdoing. Now think of those who are Luminaries who have sought to divert attention from their failure by opening up a new front. "What we need is a new Family Values Task Force to teach every child in America..." or some such nonsense.
- A secondary Entrepreneur will throw more opportunities at a problem instead of embracing the disciplines to approach today's problem. If a business is not going well because of lack of management, a poor business case, or inadequate marketing... start another one! "I know we have a few problems in finishing our first product, but there is a world of opportunity for a second product range that we have to jump on, now!"
- A secondary Manager will institute more policies, procedures and processes when the situation calls for something else. When you have inadequate sales because your customers are leaving you to go to competitors, the bad-day-Manager implements a stricter expense control policy for the sales people. "People aren't working enough hours. Institute a punch card system so that we can know whether people are actually working." Never mind the fact that people work flexible hours, work from home, and come in on weekends; the underlying issue is that Mr. Manager wants control.
- A secondary Organizer will get into frantic firefighting mode on things that are probably not the main issue. If the situation requires a steady hand at the tiller and the

secondary Organizer is having a bad day, they will take a new tack that requires lots of activity so as to avoid the proper course of action. A chronic pattern of the dark side of an Organizer is someone who cannot stand to see a calm situation; they toss bombs into calm ponds just so that they can feel useful in remedying the ensuing chaos. "Yes, I know it's the annual planning meeting, but we have a crisis with the data security system and it could bring our whole company down if I don't get involved in fixing it."

- A secondary Networker who gets into difficulty will tend to schmooze his way out of trouble. Let's say that someone is an Entrepreneur with a secondary Networker wiring: on a bad day they will fail to apply rigor to screening opportunities, will leave people hanging, will fail to share bad news, and will float on to new relational opportunities instead of completing the ones they already have in front of them. "The difficulties with the ABC Account? Well, I met with some wonderful people (new of course) that could be great customers... maybe even a potential partner. They have an intergalactic opportunity with enormous budgets and lots of people already on board, and they are committed to working with us."

The second slice of our LEMON (and some of us have well developed slices in more than two areas) is designed to complement our primary slice. It is there for our good. Just beware of the cautions of defaulting to the dark side when you are having a bad day. When you are living under pressure, when your margin erodes, you will hear "come to the dark side" more frequently. Vince Lombardi said, "Fatigue makes cowards of us all." It also makes us dark-side-LEMONs. There is something, however, that goes beyond a dark day.

Spotting LEMONs gone sour

You may be saying, "I know someone who isn't just having a bad day, they are having a bad life! They continually display the weaknesses of their primary LEMON slice."

Where someone is routinely operating out of the weaknesses of what should be their strength then this is an indication that they are a LEMON gone sour. They have crossed a line for some reason, and it is hard to bring them back to being positive, productive, healthy and happy corporate citizens. Observe people around you who were thinking of leaving a job, leaving a marriage, getting an undesirable teenage boyfriend, or somehow straying from a path called reasonable. As Johnny Cash knew, "The line" is something you can almost see, and you can also see when someone is flirting with the line.

Surely if we understand who we are and how we are wired then we can avoid crossing the line? Surely we can avert major fallout and redeem bad leadership situations? This would be true if we didn't each bring a past to the table that causes dysfunctional behavior where we go into TILT mode, and our lights dim, and our emotions shut down, and the game is over. To avoid this we should consider just what it is that pushes each of the LEMONs over the line.

The principle of alignment

To provide some rationale for why LEMONs run out of grace in a particular context, we have to examine another truism.

LEMON TRUISM: When things are out of alignment with what we believe to be truth, then eventually it wears away at our core.

You don't have to be a philosopher to have a view of how the world works. Each of us has a set of assumptions, which we believe are true, about how the world works. Our family, culture, belief system and education help shape these presuppositions.

People have given different labels to what is generally called worldview:

- Weltanschauung – Immanuel Kant
- Mental model of the world – Toffler
- Sense of how the world works – Sowell
- Conceptual scheme – Nash
- Basic cognitive orientation – Mulder
- "A set of assumptions held consciously or unconsciously in faith about the basic make up of the world and how the world works" – Darrow L. Miller

In addition to our view of how the world works, we also have a set of values that we live by if we are true to ourselves. People value things like honesty, trust, relationship, hard work, creativity, education, relationships, and the list goes on. All of these things, taken together, shape what causes us to be comfortable and effective in different situations.

What we often fail to add into the mix—in fact, I have never seen it covered elsewhere—is our leadership type, yet this has a profound effect on whether we succeed in a situation over the long term. It determines whether we can have sustainable impact. Why? This takes us to another truism.

LEMON TRUISM: When we have to work in a manner that is inconsistent with who we are, we cannot have sustainable impact.

Stated another way, if things, over time, become out of alignment with our view of the world we either need to change our worldview, or we need to move on. Sometimes these battles of worldview are quite public. In the corporate world, it is the opposition of the family of the founders to the new directions of management at Disney or Hewlett Packard. In the football arena it is the differences between the front office and the coaching staff that causes the coach to leave. At the baseball stadium it is the decision to part ways despite winning performances on the field, and the inevitable "citing irreconcilable differences" quote in the newspaper.

Easy ways to get LEMONs out of alignment

Luminaries have often created the ideas that are the foundation of the company: if you want to see them misaligned and ineffective, simply ignore their ideas. If the ideas are too good and will not go away, overlook the Luminary who had a huge part to play and ascribe everything to corporate genius. If this doesn't work, discredit the ideas. If you can get away with it, steal ideas and rename them. This will suck the life out of a Luminary. I recently observed a situation where a company received government approval on a particular medical technology, and the man who held the patents and had led the team doing the inventions was pretty much ignored. What a shame.

For Entrepreneurs, you can easily alienate them by committing one of the more common crimes of our time: the automatic replacement of the founders of organizations with "professional management." Don't bother to grow them; tell them that they don't have what it takes to lead to organization to the next level. If you have an ounce of compassion and don't want to see them totally discouraged, dangle some capital and a new opportunity carrot in front of them. Tell them how you need their energy and enthusiasm to start a new venture. Tell them that (if they sleep on the office floor and eat junk food for three or five years) it could be big. Pick them up like a corporate lab rat and place them on the next treadmill. You wouldn't want to see that raw talent wasted.

Managers take longer to die, so your safe strategy is to always have them in a support role. Tell them they are progressing nicely, but never give them a shot at the main job. You could even string them out by complimenting them on their improvement, but suggest that they need to change a few things like their interpersonal skills or capacity to envision... something vague that is hard for them to accomplish. Eventually they will leave and become a fine CEO somewhere else, but you won't have to deal with them. If that strategy doesn't work, another way to drive off a Manager is to acknowledge privately the changes needed to improve the organization, but do the opposite in public. Eventually your statements about reality will be so at odds with their's that they will do the polite thing and leave.

The quickest way to kill an Organizer is to disconnect them from the key leader whom they were serving. This is best done by inserting a layer of management in between them and the person they signed up to support. Pretty soon you will hear them say the key phrase, "There is a lack of integrity in the organization." What it really means is, "I feel dislocated from key leaders, and I cannot function well without close contact to decision-makers because I lose my context." If you want proof that this happens, count the number of kiss and tell books on the market where a supporter of a public figure has been alienated and then told all. It is much easier to alienate the Organizer than help them grow to the next level. The Organizer must own some of this problem because it is easier for an Organizer to take offense than expand beyond instinct.

Having laid our hand on the extensive Rolodex of the Networker, the next thing to do to make them ineffective is to exclude them from the inner circle. Let them know that we need more concrete skills in the executive team... you know, people who can do things. If they don't get discouraged by this—they can be optimistic— then point out that the box of "hot leads" "new prospects" and "great partners" they brought to the table had more flakes than your breakfast cereal. Make sure that they know they are being groomed to go, not to grow. Ask, "What have you done for me lately?" And don't forget to frequently change the compensation package in your favor should the Networker start to do well.

None of us really needs any advice about how to build ourselves up by putting others down. My hope is that by seeing it stated this bluntly we will overcome the twin urges to victimize others and feel like a victim ourselves. Avoid your dark side, and don't push others to theirs.

My Sour LEMON profile
On a bad day, I am:

L	E	M	O	N

Chapter 15
Problems when we fail to understand LEMON Leadership

*L*imited definitions of leadership types – as opposed to the abundant definition of styles – has led to a variety of ills.

I am a failure

Many competent but different leaders have come to think of themselves as failures simply because they cannot squeeze themselves into the canned definitions of Managers and Entrepreneurs. If they are not Managers then they incorrectly classify themselves as Entrepreneurs when, in reality, they are risk averse. Worse, they label themselves "support people" and downplay their leadership contribution. The more typical scenario is that the organizational culture is Manager-dominant in that this is the leadership type most easily understood and valued as the safe bet. Within this environment Luminaries (unhappily) allow themselves to be labeled as "visionaries" which, in the eyes of a Manager-led culture, is one step away from loony. These visionaries get exiled to an office that has minimum passing traffic so that they can "be undisturbed in their creativity" which really means "cause the least damage." Organizers get dragged out of their cubicles in a crisis, but they are seldom given real leadership jobs because they "lack the finesse of a true leader" (i.e., Manager). Networkers are celebrated when they are making sales, but are mostly viewed as empty suits who do a lot of talking, and are best sent to the glue factory should they miss their quota. Even worse, if they stay around and get elevated to positions of authority, they become an annoyance in that they freely "borrow" the stories of others and parlay them into their own success. But few organizations say, "What we need at this stage of our corporate lifecycle, in this phase of our industry, is a Networker… and these are the implications for the rest of us." The net result is that Entrepreneurs are good for start-ups, but when the real business of managing gets underway, the Luminaries, Entrepreneurs, Organizers and Networkers are under utilized, and secretly feel like failures. This is a huge waste of human capital.

Killing the corporation to avoid other LEMONs

Another consequence of failing to understand different leadership types is the failure not just of a leader, but also of an entire organization. I first met George when he was contemplating folding – simply closing down – a successful business. He was smart, hard working, and highly regarded in his specialty. His profits had grown to a point where he was quite comfortable. Yet he was willing to take the radical step of closing down his company because he saw no way of dealing with someone else on the management team whose behavior exasperated him. There were some complicating factors, but a key issue was that this other person had a different leadership type, and he did not recognize the implications of mixing his and her leadership types in a small company. In a larger corporation I have seen corporation-wide paralysis because of an incomplete understanding of leadership types that led to a CEO and a President ending up in seemingly irreconcilable positions. The trickle-down effect of this was devastating to the functioning of the executive team and ultimately the stock price.

LEMON TRUISM: Most organizations hire leaders; few grow them.

In those companies where the organization itself transcends individual leaders such that the company itself is not at risk, breakdown of relationships is often the result of failing to recognize different leadership types. After early successes, leaders come to suspect each other and question the value added by other executives. I have seen numerous situations where executives confide that "they are the ones doing the real work" while their colleagues are coasting.

Looking at this point from another angle, when there is a change of leadership, the "new brooms" syndrome breathes life into the executive management function, for a while. But over time, the supporting leaders can commit equal but opposite errors - you could call them the sabotage and pedestal strategies.

- They come to take the leadership assets of the main leader for granted, and then the behavior of the team begins to undermine the essence of the primary leader. This, in turn, leads to a diminishing effectiveness of that leader, and a spiraling self-fulfilling prophecy takes effect. (Note that I use the word primary because I inherently believe that leadership is at once an individual and a team reality.)

- Alternately, they place the leader on a pedestal where he or she can do no wrong. This, of course, underplays the gifting of the supporting leaders and demagoguery emerges.

Of course, the key leader can place him/herself on the pedestal and believe his/her own advertising a tad too much. They assume that their brilliance got them where they are, others disagree... then the cycle repeats itself.

Cheaper to buy LEMONs

Most organizations can hire leaders; relatively few can grow them. Fewer still can grow leaders across the spectrum of leadership types. The makeup of organizations tends to result in their valuing one leadership type over another. The not-so-subtle result is that the remaining leadership types are not just under-valued, but devalued. I worked with an organization some years ago that had no Luminaries or Entrepreneurs on the team: they used to have them, but they chased them off when they decided to "go corporate."

The incompleteness of traditional leadership models reinforces this scenario where few organizations are systematically growing leaders. This is hugely expensive because it is, in fact, not only cheaper but more effective to grow LEMONs (in the corporate setting) than to buy them. Risk is radically reduced when you know the soil and the environment and the work history of your next leader. Plus it is a loud statement that you have a culture that nurtures the leader within the people in your organization.

Transition time: Leadership Tollbooths

I have spent some time in and around Jakarta. Like New Jersey, toll roads are the rage. When you pass through the toll booths there is a price to pay. When organizations transition leaders they have to pass through the leadership tollbooth. The less you have groomed leaders within the corporation, the higher the price you pay at the tollbooth. Research indicates that the more successful leadership transitions are in corporations that promote from within. Even so, transition from one chief executive to another is difficult. It is all the more painful if the organization does not recognize where there is a change in leadership types involved in the CEO transition. I worked with an organization that had a 25-year history of taking leaders from the supply room to the front lines of leadership, quickly. At the senior echelons of leadership, however, leadership transitions were at less than rocket speed. Further, the organizational culture allowed "followers" to both keep and be verbal about emotional attachments to past leaders. As the CEO role switched from a Luminary to a Networker, there was no formal addressing of what these changes would mean to the organization. For five years the new leader strove to establish his leadership against the backdrop of staff feeling that he was "never quite matching up to the Luminary."

There are some negative patterns of transition that flatten tollbooths or cause leaders to get their inflated vehicles stuck in the narrow gate. These are exacerbated by a failure to understand the five core types of leaders:

- Founders (often Entrepreneurs) cannot transition key functions to Managers because they cannot imagine how their passion can be sustained in a world of process and corporate discipline.
- Luminaries cannot see their limits and hand off to Managers who can take the idea and build an organization in support of it.
- Managers fail to see a declining organization in need of

Luminaries, Networkers and Entrepreneurs, so they drive it into the ground by doing more of what got them into trouble in the first place.

- Organizers cannot imagine a steady progression in an environment of calm, a world without daily crises, a clean minefield.
- Networkers don't believe that others have the same feel for the relational intangibles that make the business more than nuts and bolts.

Any leader can have a hard time letting go unless they have a healthy self-assessment. In these days of Public Relations where few leaders are as good as their press copy, it is hard for them, having walked in places of power, to go back to the grass hut. Just ask past presidents.

Chapter 16
LEMON Vision

*I*t is not very helpful to say that effective leaders envision the future. Unless you know the difference between each type of leader and what this does to their view of the future, that's about as useful as saying that effective glasses have lenses.

The key is to find out what the lenses of LEMONs do to their view of the future so that when they speak we can understand. The fact is that vision for an Organizer is radically different from Vision for a Luminary. Neither is more right than the other; they are just different. If we miss this we will try to squeeze leaders into the vision tube and will completely miss the fact that there is more than one or two types of vision.

Debunking the visionary myth

Many people have not lived out their full potential because they believe the myth that only some leaders are visionaries. You can hear the evidence of this faulty thinking if you listen in on the average conversation about leadership. "He's a real visionary." The result is that many have excused themselves from the role of leader citing the "fact" that they do not have vision as proof that they are not leaders. In this chapter my goal is to affirm you by demystifying the notion of vision and showing you that every leader has vision, it just looks different depending on one's leadership DNA.

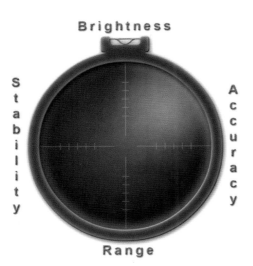

"Visionary" is not some separate kind of leader. Were this true the book would be titled VENOM Leadership with the subtitle, *How to kill your followers before they kill you,* or something along those lines. In fact, in the high tech companies in Silicon Valley the label of visionary often means "had some good ideas once, but we had to move him aside so we could actually get things done." When people start calling you the company visionary, beware. Next they will be locking you away in a corner far from the real action of the organization.

So let's take a gander at vision as seen through the eyes of each leader. I like to think of vision using the metaphor of binoculars or sites. The four dimensions to vision which I have chosen are:

1. **Brightness**: how clear is the vision, how fresh, how "breakthrough." As the saying goes, "The simple strive to be profound; the profound strive to be clear."
2. **Range**: how far will the vision take us into the future. A friend, Graham Power, has a 100 year plan for his business. My personal range is about five to ten years ahead of things actually happening. This isn't good or bad, simply a fact of my leadership wiring.
3. **Accuracy**: one can have luminescence and range and be mistaken. So one has to get a sense of how well one is calibrated. In earlier discussions about Managers, I called this "The Reality Index."
4. **Stability**: having perfectly clear sights that reveal things for 9 miles with great accuracy is useless if you cannot hold steady. You might call this the "groundedness" or "earthiness" of vision.

Luminary vision

One of my favorite stories is of the cathedral in England that took generations to complete. At the same time as they built it, the early fathers planted a forest that would be ready when the rafters needed replacing 400 years hence. I don't know what team of players was involved in that decision; what I suspect, however, is that there was a Luminary in the mix.

Vision to a Luminary is long-range. It has become less than popular in the business world to develop five and ten year plans. In some industries that are capital intensive and have long lead times, a one-year planning horizon is too short. For some people, a one-year window is likewise too short. Sure things happen in the everyday, but the really important things can hinge on an instant but take decades to evolve. The mind of a Luminary does not have too much trouble thinking in multiple generations. The vision of Luminaries can take a complex array of variables into account, although the distillation of them all should lead to something that is simply profound. Putting a man on the moon is simple, yet profound. Placing millions of transistors in a silicon chip is a simple vision with many inherent complexities. Taking hundreds of thousands of genes and placing them on a cheap chip is simply brilliant.

Vision to a Luminary is also far-sighted. One can have a long planning horizon without being far-sighted, but on a good day, a Luminary is also far-sighted. Luminaries need glasses to see things up close, not on the horizon.

While there are doubtless exceptions to this (such as the myopic genius who has a narrow field of study), Luminaries find joy in formulating vision that spans diverse disciplines, organizations, industries, societies and even nations. The key to such vision is integration. The Luminary thinks through the organizing principles that are true across these domains and therefore provide synthesis or integration. The founding of "universities" comes from the premise that everything is part of and fits logically into a greater whole, the universe.

The temptation of concrete, pragmatic people is to write off the vision of a Luminary as airy-fairy, conceptual and of no earthly use. Don't be so quick. Remember the answer given by the Chinese man when asked by the Frenchman what he thought of the French Revolution: "It's too soon to tell."

"I have a dream…" – that is Luminary vision.

Type of Leader	What they see	What they don't see
L**U****M****I****N****A****R****Y**	The future as now	The detail it will take to get from here to there
	Things happening quickly - speed	Why there need to be delays
	Why something just has to happen	Why things might go wrong
	Three strategies for every situation	Reasons why they can't all be done at once
	Endless possibilities	Limited resources

Entrepreneur vision

There is a shorter fuse on the vision of an Entrepreneur. If they fail in the near-term, then they fail. The fact that their success depends on being results oriented causes them to plan in shorter increments. When Entrepreneurs have long-term vision it often starts with short-term milestones and evolves to the longer term. Isn't this true for everyone? No. Luminaries and Managers start at the long-term view and then drop down to short-term view; Entrepreneurs and Organizers start with the short-term and then expand out to the long-term perspective.

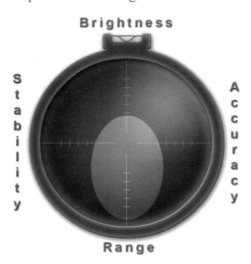

196

When considering the scope of vision, Entrepreneurs do not care as much about what happens outside their immediate competitive environment unless it has an affect on their ability to succeed. The vision of an Entrepreneur is generally confined to their organization, their locality, their industry and their term of office.

Manager vision

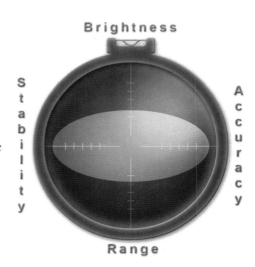

Vision to a Manager is a progressive building that comes from faithful execution of proven tasks over a medium to long-term horizon. The language of political leaders in describing the long path to eliminating terrorism smacks of the vision of a Manager. It could be paraphrased as, "I have a long term goal, and if I do the basic blocking and tackling day in and day out, without wavering, I will eventually meet my objective." To other LEONs it may not sound exciting, but to a Manager it sounds right. To the others it sounds pedestrian, but to the Manager it is predictable, and in the end it is the results that count, not the excitement of the vision. Managers have a steadier hand on the tiller than Entrepreneurs and Luminaries. (While Luminaries may actually be pretty consistent in their broad themes, the endless streams of strategies to get to the vision can cause a tacking back and forth rather than a direct "straight for the finish line" approach of the Manager.)

Organizer vision

Vision to the Organizer looks like a collection of short-term victories strung together in a story. This is not derogatory, simply factual. You cannot feed an Organizer a line about something that will happen 10 years from now and not give them some near-term wins to hang onto. "Our goal is to have the best football franchise in the NFL ten years from now." This will not sit well with an Organizer.

Vision to an Organizer and a Networker has more "feel" words than "see" words. "My vision is to create an organization that is buzzing, excited, executing effectively in the midst of chaos." "My vision is of a dynamic, nimble, agile organization that stays two steps ahead of our hungry competitors."

The required reading for an Organizer includes books with words like "chaos," "paranoid," "agile," and "crisis."

Organizers spell planning this way: B-O-R-I-N-G.

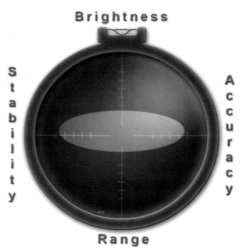

If your boss or your wife or your colleague is an Organizer and you are a LEM (or some combination thereof) make sure that you give them some near term victories in the plan, something that they can check off and say, "We did it!" before they are in a wheelchair.

I have observed organizations run by Organizers, and the people are confused as to what the vision really is. They don't know because the organizer hasn't articulated it. You can have the same organization led by a Luminary, Entrepreneur, Manager or Networker, and the leader would have given enough clues to enable their followers to get a handle on the vision. But an

Organizer is different. Unless they have a strong secondary slice that they lean into, they run the risk of sailing a confused ship. Others don't know where they are going, so they cannot get around the Organizer to adequately support them. This is a serious downside of unconscious competence, not knowing one's leadership type, and failing to translate for the crew the operating implications of having an Organizer at the helm.

Networker vision

The vision of a Networker involves a series of connected dots where the dots can be people, partners, companies or organizations. Sometimes they can be a series of events or meetings. Networker vision is usually flexible with space for adding in new things and opting out of other things. It is fluid, not rigid, and filled with the possibility of the spontaneous.

Brightness

Stability

Accuracy

Range

One of the ways I know whether someone is a Networker is by watching how they formulate vision. Networkers formulate vision on the road. Their organizations are sometimes fearful every time they return from a trip because they may have picked up a new vision along with the flu germs on the plane. Many Networkers borrow and tweak the vision of others more than creating their own. To them, of course, it is their own.

A word of caution to Networkers: Do not to let your vision be the vision of the last person who came through your office. Develop a disciplined approach to assimilating and weighing inputs without losing the power of your spontaneity.

Beware of borrowed vision

People "get vision" in different ways. There is usually some agitating factor such as competition, economic changes, peer encouragement, regulatory changes, or inspiration. There is also a vision pendulum that swings between "I created it myself" and "I borrowed it from someone else." Once again, it follows the LEMON pattern where a Luminary is more likely to have freshly inspired vision, and a Networker is more likely to borrow from, lean into, affirm, and modify vision initiated by others.

> **LEMON TRUISM: There is a vision pendulum that swings between "invented here" and "borrowed."**

While this may be seen as a caution for Networkers, the extremes are a caution for all leaders. There is, after all, "nothing new under the sun." All leaders are shaped by many factors, and the point here is to recognize how you, given your leadership type, respond to stimuli that cause you to envision. Are you an isolated Luminary, a market-driven Entrepreneur, a circumstance-instructed Manager, a quick-success Organizer, or a borrowed-this-from someone Networker? And how could you season your natural tendencies with slices of the other leaders?

Is timing everything?

When we fail to put time into visioning, we don't have a continual shaft of sunlight that drives away the mists of the moment. And when our own vision is misty, we grasp for someone else's vision, give it a twist, and in the worst-case scenario, we play politics and give the unsuspecting vision-donor a bad twist too.

The bigger downside of borrowed vision is that we don't see the full organizational implications of the vision, and we end up with a huge disconnect between the stated vision and the practical operation of the organization.

It gets worse when your LEMON profile doesn't match that of the leader whom you emulated. So if you get your vision from airline magazines or the last person who came through your office, make sure that you submit it to a team that includes the full LEMON so that together they can test it and figure out its implications.

My LEMON vision

I envision like a ...   L   E   M   O   N

Mark out your own vision on the chart   provided in the Appendix.

Chapter 17
The Full LEMON

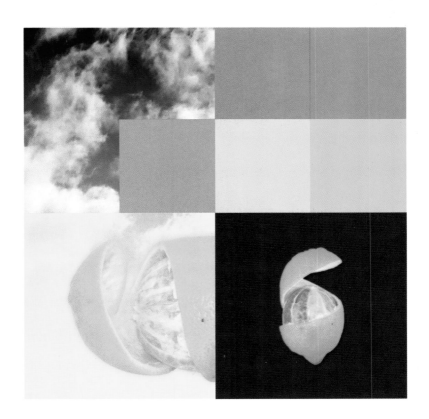

*T*ruths that make a difference are those that are good for eternity. A test of whether this model has value would be to consider it in regards to leaders through history and see how they would have been described using The LEMON Leadership Model.®

Dial up the LEMON in you

How do I put this to work? When in a situation that looks different from one in which my natural traits work well, I determine what type of leader would do best and say to myself, *"Dial up the _____, Brett."* For example, if I am meeting with a fiery-eyed business leader who is sharing the excitement of his newfound startup I say, "Dial up the Entrepreneur, Brett." Or when my best friend, the Networker, has invited me to the umpteenth meeting with a "senior leader" with whom I am sure to have a "special connection" and I arrive to find three junior leaders in the room who have just met each other for the first time… dial up the Networker. Or when I am at a conference having given a speech and people want to connect afterwards, I suppress the non-Networker tendencies.

> **LEMON TRUISM: Different situations call for different leaders; we can learn to exercise the leadership gifts of the appropriate LEMON in any circumstance.**

Perhaps there is a minor family crisis—a broken limb, a poison oak outbreak, a late school project… at this point no one cares about the fifteen year arthritic outlook of repeated bone breaks, how reading the posted signs and sticking to the paths could have prevented contact with the shrub about which they had been warned, or how we could make money reselling science projects. Save the white paper, keep your operating manual, hold the business idea: the child needs an Organizer who will help, get them to the emergency room, or pull an all-nighter. Dial up the Organizer in you.

Let's just say I am a NOE in that order (without any L or M). The setting is a meeting with friends who are considering a few community projects and micro enterprises. We (note how I became "we" pretty quickly) could start a few businesses, sponsor some orphans, paint some buildings, connect local entrepreneurs to First World markets… we could pick any number of action items and make a huge difference. I invited lots of people, and 12 have arrived for the meeting. My Networker side is relieved that so many people are in this with me, because between us we are bound to have some good things happen. My Entrepreneur side realizes that I am gathering a critical mass of resources that will enable me to pick one or two areas and get a quick win that will fuel the rest of the project. With my living room full of people I begin by welcoming everyone and saying,

> "My name is Noe, and I am excited about a new service project with opportunities to help the poor. I don't really have an agenda for this meeting so I thought we could just create an agenda together and list all the things we could do in the community. Later we can brainstorm them. Matt will take notes on his notebook computer."

As I look at one of my more structured, command-and-control colleagues next to me I am secretly thinking,

> "Watch how to make a meeting fun, buddy. None of this structure and rigor and Robert's Rules for Meetings. People are going of have a blast! I will show you how a NOE runs a meeting."

But after a minute or two the boring questions start surfacing: Mike looks uncomfortable with the brainstorming and says,

> "Before we get too deep into the list, could we discuss the real purpose of our involvement in this community, and specifically what the long term objective is?"

I think to myself, "I knew he was a Luminary or Manager… I just want to help these people, and he wants to talk about a meaningless piece of paper with plans on it."

We overcome that bump in the road because the redhead next to him fortunately suggests a stream of quick business opportunities we could work on. "Now we are talking," I think to myself. But she doesn't stop talking, and soon her few business ideas have expanded to healthcare, and education, and outside employment agencies. I think,

> "Doesn't she have any focus? At least she is excited, I suppose."

Then on my left, Matt the note taker has a question or three.

> "What is the percentage of unemployment, the annual income, and the ratio of day workers to fulltime employees? Where do they work?"

I think, but don't say, "Who cares? We are here to discuss a few opportunities to get something done quickly!" But Matt is not going away.

> "And do we know the percentage of disposable income spent inside versus outside the community?"

A few people are nodding sagely at Matt's question, and this irks me.
> "I know someone who could buy some of the community's arts and crafts" says Nora,
> "And I am happy to go around and see if some local stores will buy them: I can even put in some money to get samples made," says Edna.

I, Noe, think, "Finally, we have some real work getting done."

While I am affirming Nora and Edna for their ideas, I notice Martha's temperature has risen fifteen degrees in less than a minute. I am glad I have lots of N-O in me because I can spot her unease.

"What is it, Martha?" I ask.
She wants to know,

> "Do we think it is responsible for us to be giving them money without more guidelines? What are our funding criteria?"

One step forward, two steps back. As the hours tick by we have grown the list, Matt has injected a few categories for our thoughts and vainly attempted to insert order into the discussion periodically. Then Olive semi-explodes.

> "I am so frustrated. For three hours we have talked about having meetings to figure things out. I was excited when I came, but we have gone backwards... I will personally do these two things."

She is expressing what I am feeling. Later in the kitchen we commiserate with each other and talk about how we will just do some things ourselves. We can't stand the thought of more meetings.

What could have been done differently in handling this meeting? First, given that the team knew each other quite well before the meeting, Noe should have remembered that five of the attendees were predominantly Managers. Next, he should also have known that there were one or two Luminaries in the group. So more than half the group would predictably be interested in the broader context of the meeting, and Noe could not realistically have expected to get through five or seven minutes without someone asking about the big picture.

Second, given that Noe didn't have a Luminary bone in his body, he might have asked Leonard the Luminary to take five minutes to paint the broad picture around where things might be heading with the community project in the next two or three years. This would also have helped set the context. With so many Managers at the meeting, Noe should have had a semblance of order and given a rough agenda, even if it was only sketched out on a flipchart. Third, he could have stated that a detailed plan would be prepared later, thereby assuring the Managers that their hot button was not overlooked. Fourth, for the Organizers in the room, it would have helped to have a running Issues Log (once again visible to all) so that potential problems could be noted and the group could have moved on to more productive things. Finally—Entrepreneurs and Networkers need things too—the agreed business opportunities could have been noted on a flipchart. The whole meeting, while not to Noe's free-flowing liking, would have been better for everyone. What did Noe fail to do? He did not think about what each person needed in order to be effective in making their contribution; he didn't put himself in their shoes; he didn't defer to their wiring, thereby failing to serve them and the project. The message to Noel would be: Dial up the LEMON. The alternative: only invite NOEs to the meeting.

> **LEMON TRUISM: Growth comes through recognizing, appreciating and affirming the "other" leadership types—the ones that are not our primary and secondary slices.**

A Leader for all Seasons

There are also different seasons in one's personal life and career that call for a different type of leader. There are times when the troops need a morale boost, and they need someone who can genuinely feel their pain and empathize with their difficulties. Dial up the Networker. There are situations that call for meticulous planning and attention to detail: switch hats and become a Manager. When immediate action is needed and the job must get done now, become more of an Organizer. When focus, energy and resource gathering are key, dial up the Entrepreneur. When there are long-term implications of today's decisions, take the Luminary posture and deal with the assumptions behind the decision.

Regardless of your faith persuasion, the historical person of Jesus Christ is an interesting test case for the theory of becoming a five-slice-LEMON. Whether you like him or not, it has been convincingly argued that his teaching is the basis of law, governance and ethics in much of the world. There is certainly evidence for him being a moral person and a great teacher. Whether or not you would go so far that his claims to be God were true, his contemporary religious critics and Roman rulers had a tough time pinning any wrongdoing or crime on him. So it stands to reason that not only did he have good teaching, but he also walked the talk. His rich and colorful life makes it worth examining to see how well he fared in exhibiting the right kind of leadership in differing circumstances.

Situation	How Jesus led	What he left to others
He taught crowds the principles of living life in what is called "the Sermon on the Mount."	He was a Luminary in this situation; he shared the principles, challenged previous viewpoints, and laid a foundation for tackling many of life's big issues.	He left it to others to figure out the practical outworking of the teaching in their context. He said, for example, that we should love others as we love ourselves. Over the centuries people figured out what this means for things such as human rights, women's rights and justice systems.

Situation	How Jesus led	What he left to others
He launched a new movement, recruited people, and secured funding from unconventional sources.	Here he was an Entrepreneur. He selected good people (eleven out of twelve isn't bad) and set up a traveling service model. On the funding side, there is some speculation that he self-funded by stashing away cash when running the carpentry shop (his prior work experience). Or perhaps Joe and Mary had invested some of the seed money that the traveling Iraqi think tank (also knows as the Wise Men) had endowed him with at birth. That too is speculation. What we do know is that a band of women (with little to no status in those days) provided him and his startup group with funding.	He let a group of women get involved and invest some sweat equity. This paid off because when his remaining 11 recruits bailed out, the investors stuck with him. (He said something about the connection between treasure and heart.) He didn't turn down their financial assistance and logistical support for the operation. He utilized their accommodations and benefited from their catering. He mobilized a cross-section of people and let them do what they did best.

Situation	How Jesus led	What he left to others
He instituted processes for the core business of his venture: preaching, teaching, healing the sick, feeding the hungry, etc. He developed longer-term marketing strategies, and had a rollout plan in mind for how he would spread the operation geographically. He also taught how to focus on one market first (the Jews) and then get into customer/market segmentation (such as Samaritans, Gentiles and men, women and children.)	He developed leaders, trained by example, and delegated tasks to those whom he had trained. He watched them do what he had taught them, and then he sent them out to work in teams without him. He risked giving them new territories, and gave specific operating instructions about where to stay, what to take with them, how to relate to potential customers, and what to offer people. Later he asked for a report back on their activities and was as interested in their development as he was in what they had accomplished. He was an excellent Manager.	He didn't do what they could do for themselves. In this and other instances he challenged them to do what they could do rather than do everything for them. For example, when his followers reported a major food shortage at an outdoor event, he said, "You feed them." He quickly transitioned from "show and tell" to delegation. After just three years he delegated responsibility and authority to his leadership team for the whole enterprise. This was entrepreneurial, and also managerial in development processes he had implemented.

Situation	How Jesus led	What he left to others
His followers had gone back to their old jobs. Jesus came to find them and re-commission them. They had been out in a fishing boat all night, so he did the practical thing and made a fire, procured (or otherwise obtained) some fish, and put on a breakfast for 12 people.	This was Jesus the Organizer at work. He saw a practical need and filled it. He did the same thing when he and the lads had come in from a busy day and were about to eat a big dinner, but there was no servant on hand to wash their dirty feet, so he did the job himself. The situation didn't call for a lecture on podiatry (L) or a back-of-the-napkin business plan (E) or Standard Operating Procedures for foot washing (M) or for a phone call to someone who washes feet (N). It called for someone to strip off their clothes, get a bucket and a rag, and work his way around the table to clean 24 dirty feet. It needed an Organizer. He used phrases like "I have come to do" and "it is finished" and "I have completed the work."	In the short-term all they had to do was show up, eat the fish, and get their feet cleaned.

Long-term, he left them to figure out the life implications for themselves. The incident was not forgotten or its significance lost on them. |

Situation	How Jesus led	What he left to others
How Jesus recruited his followers is a lesson in networking. His first two were referrals from his cousin, John an intriguing character who ran a sort of pre-launch campaign for Jesus out in the desert. Two of John's guys heard a recommendation from John and decided to see what Jesus was up to.	Jesus invited cousin John's devotees to hang out with him for the day. One of them, Andrew, was a bit of a Networker himself. When he realized there was something special about Jesus, he promptly went home and recruited his brother, Simon, who became employee # 3. The next day Jesus followed the relational trail to the hometown of Andrew and Simon and recruited # 4, Philip. Philip then brought Nathaniel, # 5. (Actually, Jesus had been checking Nathaniel out in advance because when Nate arrived Jesus said, "One day, long before Philip called you here, I saw you under the fig tree.") We're not sure how, but he had a bead on Nathaniel's character and location.	Jesus didn't say, "Step back, you lowlifes. I can do this on my own." Check the tally: 1 and 2: referral from John 3: referral from Andrew 4: Jesus did it, but the guy was in the network of Andrew and Peter. 5: Nate, courtesy of Phil.

In my view Jesus Christ not only exercised all five LEMON slices, but he also knew when to get out of the way and let others utilize their capabilities and thereby feel even more part of the team. What's more, his ability to rapidly switch between the slices is nothing short of amazing. He defended good ideas, and he defended people from bad ideas. He protected opportunities, and he challenged people about being opportunists. He instilled processes but always made the processes serve the greater purpose (and broke processes where they were breaking people). He networked people together, and he discouraged people who shouldn't be part of the core team from coming on board. He jumped in and did menial tasks, and he corrected those who saw a practical solution as the answer to a deeper issue. He was the perfect LEMON.

We're not perfect, but we can be in process

Right about now, whether facetiously or seriously, you are probably saying, "But I am not Jesus!" Other leaders have recognized this too. In fact, Napoleon said it well:

> I know men and I tell you that Jesus Christ is no mere man. Between him and every other person in the world there is no possible term of comparison. Alexander, Caesar, Charlemagne, and I founded empires. But on what did we rest the creations of our genius? Upon force. Jesus Christ founded His empire upon love; and at this hour millions of people would die for Him.

If Jesus is at least a role model, then we should consider modeling our leadership patterns on what worked for him. Napoleon recognized that Jesus based his venture on love. There are many ways to love people. I mentioned earlier the friend who told me words to the effect that "I believe the second most loving thing I can do for one of my colleagues is confront them about leadership deficiencies." The first most loving thing to do went without saying: it is to lay down one's life for someone else. I believe there is a third way that Jesus modeled love, and that was by subjugating his rights in order to be the type of leader for which a situation called. Foot washing wasn't fun, but it was the needed loving act. For us, re-prioritizing our forward-facing

LEMON slice means suspending our leadership leanings—all of the LEMON strengths, weakness and traits we have considered—and doing what is best for others in a particular situation, even if it is not naturally who we are.

We will never be perfect, but we can follow the role models of history and learn how to lead intelligently and humbly. We can ask, "What type of leader does this situation require me to be in order than I can serve effectively?"

Twisting the LEMON

I leave you with a final thought on utilizing the principles of LEMON Leadership. You could call it LEMON Twist.

LEMON TRUISM: Success in implementing these concepts is proportional to your ability to personally twist your LEMON to put forward the right slice at the right time.

Discerning which slice is needed means suppressing our natural urges to (a) do what is most comfortable to us, and (b) react negatively to the least comfortable leadership slice. I have seen two approaches to learning how to master the art of twisting the LEMON.

The first runs the lines of the self-improvement approach. Leaders see the rationale of deferring to others, learning the value of others' gifts and talents, developing their own prowess in reflecting the multiple facets of effective leadership, and doing what makes logical sense. They learn to twist the LEMON with the twin objectives of accomplishing a set of goals in mind and their own improvement. Their premise is that if they understand something thoroughly, they will be able to master it. Their philosophy says that if they improve as a leader it will be better for those whom they lead; all boats will rise with their tide. Growth in LEMON twisting is a matter of maturing as a person.

The second group goes the heart route to twisting the LEMON. Their philosophy is that if their motivation can be genuine service, then they will twist the LEMON out of a genuine belief that this is the best way to serve. They cultivate their appreciation for what others have to bring to the table. They develop a strong belief that it is not always opportune for them to personally be the lead dog. They exercise leadership with a humility that would seem too risky to the self-improvers. They lean less into their ability to learn and master, and more into an acknowledgement of their own negative tendencies. They make a genuine appeal to see through the eyes of others what they themselves do not see. They make a choice to prefer others whenever possible. They do not believe that they can twist the LEMON without help beyond themselves.

LEMON TRUISM: The freer we are of internal hang-ups, the easier it is to twist the LEMON.

The Power of And

You will need to decide what would motive you to become an effective LEMON twister. Beyond that, you will need to learn which approach helps you to sustain LEMON twisting over the long haul. Your choice will ultimately be informed by your worldview. There is no reason why we cannot embrace both approaches simultaneously. The first approach transforms our minds, the second our ego. The power of an "and" approach is that both our minds and our hearts are renewed. Why is this important? Because the membranes that give each slice of the LEMON definition and help us have understanding about ourselves and others can become the walls of our ego if we view them as the boundaries of what makes us "right" and others "not as right."

LEMON TRUISM: When clarity about who we are succumbs to our perception of how great we are, we stifle the urge to rotate the lemon.

When ego overpowers reality we fail to rotate the LEMON as we should. The converse is also true. When we go from *either* to *and* we discover the principle of finding something through losing it, discovering a greater whole through letting go of the smaller sliver. When we are secure in who we are, why we are here and where we are going, we are free to use all five slices of the LEMON in serving others.

Appendix

YOUR LEMON PROFILE

Scores from Ch.2 - 6	L	E	M	O	N
TOTAL:	013	2	9	6	

Horizon	Nearer	⬅➡		Further
Depth of field	Small amount in focus	⬅➡		Lots in focus at once
Fuse	Long fuse	⬅➡		Short fuse
Tolerance of risk	Low tolerance for risk	⬅➡		High tolerance for risk
Regard for process	High regard for process	⬅➡		Low regard for process
Intensity	Low	⬅		High
If high intensity	Deep	⬅➡		Fast

	L	E	M	O	N
I think like a…	L	E	M	O	N
I see like a…	L	E	M	O	N
I hear like a…	L	E	M	O	N
I talk like a…	L	E	M	O	N
I like to be complimented for…	Ideas	Moving and shaking	Efficiency	Action	Being likeable
Easily connect with…	Ideas	Resources	Processes	Issues	People
In my strengths I am like…	L	E	M	O	N
My weaknesses are mostly…	L	E	M	O	N
I protect my…	Ideas	Opportunities	Systems	Freedom to act	Rolodex
I envision like a …	L	E	M	O	N
On a bad day I am a…	L	E	M	O	N
I respond to pressure like a …	L	E	M	O	N
I fight like a...	L	E	M	O	N
I take flight like a...	L	E	M	O	N
I respond well like a...	L	E	M	O	N

Supplementary Profile Information:

Thinking	Analytical	⬅➡	Intuitive
Conceptualizing	Concrete	⬅➡	Abstract
Interacting	Introvert	⬅➡	Extravert
Confronting	Direct	⬅➡	Indirect
Processing	Sequential	⬅➡	Random

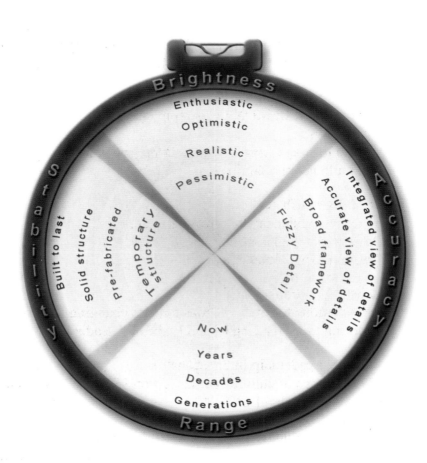

We offer presentations, forums and workshops on LEMON Leadership. The principles of LEMON Leadership are applied to specific situations, giving a tailored experience that more directly addresses your needs.

1. LEMON Leadership and Direct Sales
    Growing your business through an understanding of customers, colleagues and the corporate office.

2. Families of LEMONs
    The impact of LEMON Leadership on family dynamics.
    How to leverage LEMON Leadership principles to build healthy families.

3. LEMON Marriages
    Increasing understanding in a marriage.
    De-personalizing conflict.
    Creating new partnerships.

4. LEMONs in transition
    Consultations for organizations that are changing leaders.
    Adapting the Operating Model to the new leader.

5. LEMON Leadership International
    The influence of culture and nations on LEMON Leadership.
    Living with global LEMONs.

6. LEMONs, Values and Foundational Principles
    Aligning the type of leader, the values of the organization, and bedrock beliefs.

7. LEMON Leadership and faith-based organizations
    An exploration of the "five-fold ministries" of Ephesians and their linkages to LEMON Leadership.
    Restoring the missing slices of the LEMON in churches and faith-based organizations.